They shaped his body just as they shaped his mind and spirit. Alexander was not merely brilliant—he was beautiful—and already his whole being seemed to foretell his great destiny.

In 336 BC Philip was murdered and the
twenty-year-old Alexander was proclaimed king of
Macedonia, the most powerful nation in the Greek world.
The Greeks had grown impatient with the aggressions of
the Persians. The Greek colonies of Asia Minor, which
had been taken over by Persia, awaited deliverance.
With 50,000 men Alexander crossed the Hellespont
and entered Asia. Darius, king of the Persians,
was so sure of his own power that he made
no move to stop them.

But his generals were spoiling for a fight.
Spithridates, ruler of Ionia and Lydia, roused
the Persian cavalry. The encounter was violent.
Alexander narrowly escaped being killed. At the
day's end, however, he again seized the initiative
and the Persians were defeated.

One after another, the Greek colonies of Asia Minor
were freed by Alexander and his men. At Ephesus,
Priene, Miletus, and Magnesia, they restored
democratic rule. Alarmed, King Darius himself took
the field against Alexander, and met disaster
at Issus. He escaped, but his family and his riches
fell into the conqueror's hands.

Once Tyre and Sidon belonged to Alexander, the road
to Egypt lay open. A new city was born in the
Nile delta: Alexandria. The young king was hailed as
the "son of Ammon," the Egyptian deity. From now on
nothing was beyond his powers. At Gaugamela in
Mesopotamia he put Darius to flight again.
Abandoning all resistance, the Persians threw open
the gates of Babylon before the conqueror

As the years went by Alexander tamed Persia, Parthia,
Margiana, Arachosia, Bactria, and Sogdiana, and
at last stood at the gates of India. Its nations all
submitted to him, offering tribute and support.
Only the Indian king Porus refused to yield.
He marshaled an enormous army: two hundred
elephants and three hundred war chariots.

The battle was fierce, but Alexander was victorious.
"How do you wish to be treated?" he asked the
defeated Indian. "Like a king," said Porus.
Impressed by the man's dignity, Alexander allowed
Porus to keep his throne. With this new ally
at their side, the Macedonians planned to march
deeper into Asia. But Alexander's soldiers refused
to go on: He had at last reached the
outer limits of his empire.

CONTENTS

ALEXANDER THE GREAT
MAN OF ACTION
MAN OF SPIRIT

Pierre Briant

DISCOVERIES

HARRY N. ABRAMS, INC., PUBLISHERS

B y the 4th century BC all of Greece yearned for revenge. The cities buzzed with talk of a "war of reprisal" against their eternal enemy, Persia. There had been more than two centuries of clashes between the Greek and Persian civilizations, countless humiliating defeats—but also dazzling victories: on sea at Salamis, and on land at Plataea.

CHAPTER I
GREEKS AND PERSIANS

Despite their power, the Greek city-states had little hope of resisting the Persians. All too often their armies were overwhelmed by the forces of the Great King, as the Persian monarch was known (below left: A Persian warrior; right, a Greek soldier). The impulse to go on the offensive against them came firstly from Philip of Macedon, but above all from his son Alexander (opposite).

The Greeks in Asia rebelled

In 522 Darius I ascended the throne of the
Persian Empire, which included among its
vassals the Greek colonies along the Asian
coast. In 499 BC, with the help of Athens,
these colonies rebelled. Darius succeeded in
quelling the rebellion, but seeking revenge
for Athens's role in the uprising, he landed
an army at Marathon in Greece in 490 BC.
The Athenian infantry managed to defeat
the Persians; however, within ten years
Darius's son Xerxes was back—with the
largest military force the world had ever seen. Despite
the ferocious resistance of a small Spartan detachment
guarding the pass at Thermopylae, the Persians poured
into central Greece. A coalition of Greek city-states
mustered their warships in the bay of Salamis and
inflicted a first defeat on Xerxes, who withdrew to
Asia Minor. In 479 the army that he had left behind
in Europe met with fresh disaster at Plataea, and
the Greeks at once returned to the Greek cities of
Asia Minor.

The 5th century BC was marked by Athens's superiority

A treasurer holding an
abacus (above) notes
his calculations on the
tablet before him, as a
dignitary in Persian dress
prepares to pay his
province's taxes.

over all other Greek city-states. It was Athens that had led the fight against Persia. With its armies and war-fleets it forged a seaborne empire and sapped the Great King's strength on the coasts of Asia Minor and in Egypt. Even today the name of Pericles (who ruled Athens from 460 to 430 BC) and the remains of many buildings on the Acropolis remind us of this high-water mark of Athenian power. Why then did Greece soon ring with new calls to war and the inflammatory speeches of orators, in particular Isocrates?

"King Artaxerxes considers that the cities of Asia and the islands of Cyprus and Clazomenae are his by right"

In 386—nearly a century after the Persian defeat at Plataea—the king of Persia once more seized the political and military initiative. Artaxerxes reasserted the strength of the empire by forcing upon the Greeks a humiliating "King's Peace," which granted Persia control over Greece's eastern colonies. The leading Greek settlements along the Asian shore, such as Ephesus, Miletus, Priene, and many others, from the Black Sea to the mouth of the Nile, fell once more under Persian domination. This

The Great King, depicted on a 4th-century BC Greek vase (below), is seated on his throne, with his feet resting, Persian style, on a footstool. Alongside the Persians is a Greek, recognizable by his felt headgear and rich clothing; he may be Histiaeus, tyrant of Miletus and one of King Darius I's counselors. The scene is believed to represent the war council summoned by Darius before his Greek campaign early in the 5th century BC.

was the state of affairs against which the influential orator Isocrates and his friends railed. They called for an end once and for all to humiliation at the hands of the "barbarians." They demanded revenge for the destruction of Greek sanctuaries. The time had come to free their sister cities of Asia Minor from the renewed yoke of the King of Kings.

But for such a campaign to be successful, the Greek city-states had first to overcome their internal divisions, and second to accept one of their number as overlord and leader of military operations. For a time Isocrates, an impassioned proponent of a united Greece, looked to Athens for leadership. Soon disappointed by Athenian internal feuding, however, he was forced to consider other options. Almost as a last resort, he turned his gaze to a kingdom just north of Greece, Macedonia, long the subject of both hatred and fascination to its neighbors. In a speech delivered in 346 BC, he urged King Philip II of Macedon to set free the Greek cities of Asia, to conquer Asia Minor, and to implant there Greek colonies that would "serve as the frontiers of Greece and stand as a bulwark before us all."

Under Philip II, who became king in 359, Macedonia moved into the forefront of the Greek states

From the day of his accession King Philip seized every opportunity to cement his hold over the notoriously unruly Macedonian aristocracy. He raised a superbly trained army, thanks in particular to the financial resources (such as the gold-mines of Mount Pangaeus) made available by his recent conquests. In fact, Macedonia had been growing uninterruptedly in the direction of Asia as well as central Greece—most often at the expense of Athens and other Greek states, which were unable to muster an effective resistance to Macedonia's irresistible forward march. When he defeated a confederation of Greek states at Chaeronea in 338 BC, Philip spectacularly demonstrated his military and political superiority. For the Greek city-states, the great age of jealously guarded independence was coming to an end.

The victory also allowed Philip to assume leadership of the united Greek—or Panhellenic—crusade against Persia, as long as it furthered his own interests. He called together a conference of delegates from the Greek city-states at Corinth, where they created an alliance—the so-called Corinthian League. The participants concluded a "common peace," with each member retaining freedom and autonomy. But that freedom was restricted by clauses forbidding any political or social change within a city, and punishing any city that might seek to overthrow Philip and his successors. Philip was appointed *hegemon,* or general-in-chief, entrusted with leading the league's forces. Of the major cities, only Sparta refused to join. The official objective of the treaty was to declare war on the Persians and avenge the Greeks for the profanations committed by the "barbarians" in the temples of the Greeks. Following this decision Philip dispatched a first expeditionary force in 336 BC to liberate the cities of Asia and prepare the ground for an imminent landing by his entire army.

One of the first goals of Philip (opposite) was to unite the different small principalities around his capital, Pella, and strengthen the authority of the Macedonian monarchy. Macedonia's rise to power was marked by the embellishment of Pella, which Philip turned into one of the Greek world's major political and cultural centers by issuing gold and silver coins (thanks to the rich Thracian mines that fell into his hands) struck with the royal effigy (above), and by establishing a standing army. Its foot soldiers were recruited from the peasantry, its cavalry from aristocratic families, and its ranks were swelled by highly paid Greek mercenaries.

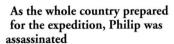

As the whole country prepared for the expedition, Philip was assassinated

At the Macedonian court lavish celebrations were underway to mark the wedding of Cleopatra, daughter of King Philip and Queen Olympias and sister of Alexander. Philip planned to

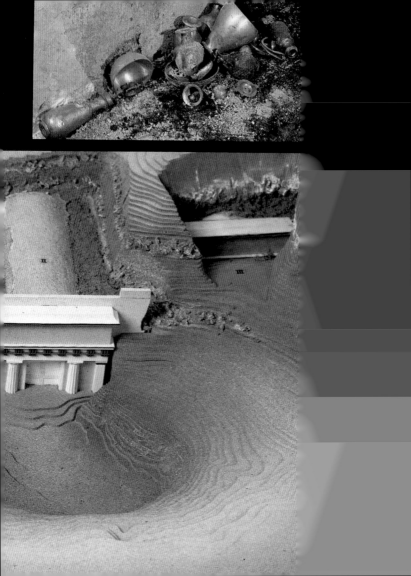

King Philip's Battle Gear?

The king found at Vergina was buried with his ceremonial weapons. Opposite: Horizontal and vertical bands of gold embellish the breastplate, which is made of fine strips of iron covered with leather and fabric. Six lions' heads glare from the front. The design allowed its wearer remarkable freedom of movement. Left: The tall-crested royal helmet, with its forehead embossed with the head of Athena, is the first Macedonian helmet ever found.

Left: A gold decorative plate of the *gorytos*, a quiver for arrows and spear, depicts the capture of a city.

attend the celebratory athletic competitions, but as he appeared at the stadium, he was struck down—and killed—by a young Macedonian nobleman, whose exact motives still remain a mystery.

His son Alexander, aged twenty, immediately succeeded Philip. Alexander appeared before the Macedonian People's Assembly for their approval. Macedonian kings were not considered absolute rulers, thus the Assembly had the right to proclaim a new king—a gesture of confirmation rather than an election. The Assembly's approval usually lent weight to the claims of an heir. Moreover, Alexander himself supervised the funeral rites in his father's honor at Aegae, an act which in Macedonian eyes constituted a symbol of dynastic continuity.

Alexander, the young heir apparent, had already proved his mettle

Like all kings' sons, Alexander was raised by private tutors. They were under the supervision of the formidable Leonidas—a relative of Alexander's mother Olympias. Leonidas was entrusted with the prince's literary and scientific instruction, as well as his physical training. Alexander led an austere life under his strict mentor, who allowed him "for breakfast, a walk before daybreak, and for dinner a light breakfast." Leonidas even rummaged through the luggage of his young charge to make sure that his mother had not

slipped in any treats for her son when he left for school. Alexander was still in his teens when he mastered the wild stallion Bucephalus, which he was to ride for nearly twenty years.

To cap his son's education, Philip called upon the renowned philosopher Aristotle, who agreed to tutor the prince in exchange for an extremely high fee. Alexander spent several years with Aristotle on the peaceful estate of Mieza near Pella, the Macedonian capital. He studied philosophy and political science, and experienced the beauties of Homer's poetry and the dramas of Euripides, while continuing his apprenticeship as king and soldier in the company of young noblemen his own age.

In 340 BC, at the age of sixteen, the young prince was considered qualified to act as regent while his father was away on military campaigns. Shortly thereafter, he himself led an army against an uncooperative Thracian people, the Maedi. In 338 he fought, with his father, against a hostile coalition of Greek city-states at the decisive battle of Chaeronea, commanding the Macedonian army's left wing. After their victory Philip sent Alexander to Athens with the ashes of the Athenian soldiers who had died in the fighting. It was his first and last opportunity to acquaint himself with a city whose cultural glories he sincerely admired.

Alexander was determined to carry out his father's plans

One of Alexander's first steps, upon assuming the king-ship, was to journey to Corinth to renew the Panhellenic

Olympias (left), Alexander's mother, was the daughter of the king of the Molossians, in the Greek republic of Epirus. Extremely strong-willed, she sought to play a political role alongside Philip (and was exiled for her efforts). She returned to Pella only at the request of her son Alexander. In later years, no matter how far his campaigns took him, he kept in close contact with her.

Far left: "One day the Thessalian Philonicus brought Philip Bucephalus, whose asking price was the [very high sum of] thirteen talents. They went down into the plain to try the stallion, and found him rebellious and utterly intractable.... When Philip impatiently gave orders to have him led away.... Alexander exclaimed, 'what a horse they are losing simply because, for want of skill and courage, they cannot exploit his virtues!' Philip addressed him: 'By thus criticizing those who are older than you, do you claim to know more than they do and to be better able to handle this horse?' 'Most certainly,' Alexander replied.... 'And if you fail, what punish-ment will you accept for your rashness?' 'By Zeus, I will pay the horse's full price!'"

Plutarch
"Life of Alexander,"
1st–2d century AD

pact of 338, and to accept the official title of general-in-chief of the detachments of the League earmarked for the Asian expedition. But his plans were delayed by the revolt of several of the Balkan peoples who periodically disrupted Macedonia's northern frontiers. As Alexander prepared for a far-off campaign, it was now, more than ever, essential to make Macedonia secure from its enemies near home.

The expedition was further delayed by a Greek insurrection. Lulled by the death of Philip II, and misled by a rumor that Alexander had died on the Balkan front, the Greek city-states set out to avenge the humiliation of Chaeronea. Their uprising was swiftly crushed by a lightning campaign directed by the young king, who besieged Thebes. The city quickly laid down its arms. With a touch of cruel humor, Alexander announced that he would leave Thebes's fate in the hands of his Greek "allies"—who elected to raze the city and enslave the surviving Thebans. Terror-stricken, the other Greek cities (including Athens, which voted to congratulate Alexander for his victories) made amends. Under the terms of the treaty signed first with Philip, then with his son Alexander, the cities of the Corinthian League sent contingents to the Macedonian king. These Greek soldiers would serve as hostages to ensure their cities' loyalty during the Asian campaign.

Keeping internal order in the huge Persian Empire required the maintenance of armies, either on a permanent or a standby basis. The Great King could call first and foremost on the palace guard, depicted (above) on the reliefs at Persepolis bearing spears and shields. In particularly serious circumstances, he could also raise military units from all the various people of his empire.

Who was this Persian adversary so often invoked by Isocrates?

In 334 the Persian Empire (which was also known as the Achaemenid Empire, after its ruling dynasty) had more than two centuries of history behind it. In fact it was around the middle of the 6th century BC that the Persian people, spurred on by King Cyrus the Great, had embarked on a conquest of the kingdoms that then made up the countries of the Middle East: Between 550 and 525 BC, the Persian army had seized the kingdom of the Medes (with its capital of Ecbatana), the kingdom of Lydia (in Asia Minor), the Neo-Babylonian kingdom (Mesopotamia and the Levant), and Egypt. By the time of Darius I, the Great, (who ruled from 522 to 490), the empire had expanded substantially in every direction.

The creation of this empire represented a profound change in the geopolitical situation in the Middle East, bringing it for the first time under the sway of the man who styled himself the king of kings— the Great King.

Standing before Darius's palace at Susa, this monumental statue (left) carved in Egypt symbolized the Great King's sway over a multitude of peoples, who are schematically characterized by costume and headdress and designated by hieroglyphic symbols (reproduced below). Upper row, left to right: Persians, Medes, and Elamites. Middle: Bactrians, Sogdians, Scythians. Bottom row: Lydians, Arabs, Egyptians. Left: Indians and Nubians.

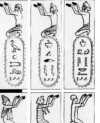

"Among so many other calamities that the city of Thebes was called upon to suffer, Thracian soldiers ransacked the house of Timoclaea, a respected woman of high moral virtue, and despoiled her of her wealth, while their leader took her by force and violated her. Then he asked her whether she possessed gold and silver hidden somewhere away. She said that she did and, leading him alone to her garden, showed him a well in which she had concealed the most precious of her goods. Then, as the Thracian bent over the well, Timoclaea pushed him in and slew him by throwing down on him a shower of stones. The Thracians led her in chains before Alexander, who at once saw from her appearance and demeanor that she was a distinguished and most courageous woman, for she followed those leading her without either fear or distress. The king asked her who she was. 'I am the sister of Theogenes,' she answered, 'who fought against Philip for the freedom of Greece and who fell at Chaeronea where he was commander in chief.' Admiring her response and her dignity Alexander ordered that she and her children be set free."

Plutarch
"Life of Alexander,"
1st–2d century AD

Broad highways allowed the Great King to communicate swiftly with the farthest-flung outposts of his empire

From western Asia Minor (Ephesus and Sardis), the Royal Road of the Achaemenid Empire ran through Ancyra (present-day Ankara), Cappadocia, the Upper Euphrates, Babylonia, and Susia. "Everywhere along it," an ancient writer reported, "are royal staging-posts and excellent hostels; it passes only through secure and inhabited regions.... From Sardis to the royal palace at Susa it measures [1,500 miles, 2,300 kilometers]; with daily stages of [15 miles, 25 kilometers], the journey takes ninety days." The empire's important cities (Babylon, Susa, and Persepolis) were linked to India and Egypt by other royal highways, traveled by the king's armies and couriers under the watchful protection of highway sentinels.

Despite setbacks following the Great King Xerxes's failure in Greece (480–79) and Athenian offensives, the empire expanded again in 334, adding huge tracts of land from Central Asia to the Persian Gulf and the whole north-south length of the Red Sea.

Egypt, which had broken away from the empire in 404, was reconquered by Artaxerxes III (who ruled from 359 to 338); the valley of the Indus, on the other hand, seems to have enjoyed a *de facto* independence. There the imperial territories were divided up into a score of provincial administrations, or satrapies, each ruled by its own satrap—a Persian word meaning "guardian of power."

Entrusted with maintaining order, the satraps commanded standing territorial forces deployed across a string of fortresses and garrisons. They were also assigned to collect taxes and tributes, which flowed into the royal treasuries and storehouses.

The satraps were local representatives of the Great King. The satrap opposite borrows imagery—the throne and parasol—from the imperial court. Below: A Persian archer.

SCYTHÆ

EUROPÆ
PARS.

Getæ

PONTVS EVXINVS.

Cerceteæ

COL
CHIS.

Choral
meni.

MARE HYRCANVM
sive CASPIVM, quod et
PONTICVM non semel a
Curtio & vocatur MAGNVM
etiam ab Arriano 3.

PAPH LAGO
NIA.

Thracibythini.

Chalybes.

Mossini.

Henetí Leuco
syri.

Amazo num

HYRC

AS

AR

MENIA.

Par
thyene.

CYPRVS

AR.

MAIOR. I

MESOPOTA
MIA.

BABYLO
NIA.

Orche
ni.

ARABIA.

AV

Chelo

MARIS
TERRANEI

MEDI
PARS.

PALÆSTINA.

LIBYÆ sive AFRI
CÆ PARS.

AEGYPTVS.

Bythemanei.

ISMAELI
TÆ.

AGARENI.

MADIAN, et
MADIANITÆ.

ZABA
DÆI,

CEDAR.

RVBRVM MARE.

ARABIÆ

ARABIA. FESICIS

PARS.

SABA.

ALEXANDRI MAGNI
MACEDONIS EXPEDITIO.

Awaiting Alexander's onslaught, the Persian Empire stretched nearly 2,500 miles (4,000 kilometers) from west to east, from Egypt to the River Indus, and 1,100 miles (1,800 kilometers) from north to south, from the Syr Darya (Jaxartes) River to the Strait of Hormuz on the Persian Gulf. It embraced infinitely diverse countries: the sandy deserts of the Iranian plateau or Egypt; the rich irrigated plains of the Nile valley, Babylonia, and Bactria; the inhospitable mountains of the Hindu Kush and the Caucasus; the Mediterranean reaches of the Asia Minor coast; the swamps of the Tigris and Euphrates deltas. Such were the landscapes Alexander would traverse. The administrative centers of the empire were linked to the different provinces by a network of highways—the Royal Roads—maintained and policed by their own bureaucracy.

The Great King's incredible wealth was rightly celebrated among the Greeks. The opulence of the royal treasuries at the time of Alexander's invasion testifies to it: The mass of gold and silver, largely unminted, that fell into his hands in the great capitals of the empire has been estimated at more than 18,000 talents—or more than 4,500 tons.

Unquestioning support of the Persian nobility furnished the Great King with administrators and generals who held his subject lands in his name. Persians were identified by their crown-shaped headgear (below).

Persian conquest had not eliminated the amazing ethnic and cultural diversity of the countries that made up the empire

The language of the conquerors, Old Persian, never spread beyond the Persian people. The Persian language was just one of the many Iranian languages spoken the length and breadth of the Iranian plateau, just as the Persians were but one of the many Iranian peoples linked by shared traditions and customs. The conquered peoples continued to use their own languages and writing forms. The Egyptians spoke Egyptian, and their scribes continued to use hieroglyphics (for inscriptions on monuments) and demotic (on papyruses). Babylonia continued to use its cuneiform script, and Greek was spoken in the colonies of Asia Minor. Even the clay tablets containing the royal archives discovered at Persepolis, the heart of the Persian Empire, are written not in Persian but Elamite, the ancient native language of the region.

And those were only the most important languages. On closer examination, the empire's linguistic pluralism is even more striking: Historians agree that in Asia Minor alone a dozen or more languages and dialects were spoken. It is true, too, that during the Persian period there was an unprecedented increase in the use of Aramaic, which eventually became the favored language of commerce and government.

After Cyrus's conquest of Media, the Median aristocracy (below) were effortlessly integrated into the empire, so much so that the word "Mede" often signified "Persian" to the Greeks.

The Great King provided a model for governing that Alexander would follow

This linguistic mosaic illustrates the extent to which local cultural traditions had been preserved. Respect for tradition was a conscious policy of the Persians, who knew that lasting power could be founded only on collaboration with local leaders.

It was a policy that the Persians also observed in respect to religion. Generally speaking, they allowed their subject peoples to practice their own faiths. Sometimes local sanctuaries were permitted special privileges. Cyrus was following this strategy when he decided in 538 BC to allow the Judaeans to leave their Babylonian exile and return to the land of their forebears, in order to build a temple there dedicated to Jehovah. Moreover, after his conquest of Babylonia, Cyrus agreed to participate in the local religious traditions, just as his successors Cambyses and Darius were revered as pharaohs

and readily agreed to offer sacrifices to the Egyptian gods. The Great Kings were well aware that they needed the support of local gods in order to rule their peoples. Alexander clearly took note of these methods for enforcing imperial rule. To a large extent, they would guide his own political choices.

Despite the diversity of his subject peoples, the Great King symbolized and perpetuated the empire's unity in his own person

The king was helped in his efforts to unify the empire by the Persian aristocracy, which had evolved into the virtual backbone of royal power in the conquered territories. All major administrative posts, high military ranks, and satrapies were almost without exception filled by representatives of the great Persian families. These Persians had also acquired lands in the empire, supplying the satraps with troops of cavalry in exchange for their estates. As they settled far and wide, the Persians of this imperial diaspora held on to their cultural and religious traditions. At Sardis in the 4th century BC a temple was erected to the great Persian god Ahura Mazda, and in every satrapy a shrine was dedicated to the goddess Anahita.

It was the political and cultural cohesion of these Persians, just as much as their devotion to the Great King and the Achaemenid dynasty, that accounted for the empire's longevity. The interests of the nobility and the ruling dynasty were thus intimately linked, for the political and economic power of the great Persian families depended on their continued domination of territories and populations. In order to control the empire, Alexander would have to establish a clear policy toward this Persian ruling class.

In the 4th century BC Greek authors depicted the Persian Empire as an institution in the throes of decay

Greek writers pointed complacently to the military deterioration of the

Persians, who had become softened, or so the Greeks thought, by the pleasures of the table and the joys of the harem; "Whoever seeks to make war on the Persians," wrote one, "may, without fighting, stroll at his ease about the country"! From the time of the wars with Persia, the intrinsic superiority—moral, political, military—of the Greeks over the "barbarians" had becoming a founding myth among the framers of Greek history.

In fact, however, the Great King could at any time amass substantial armies, and his financial resources were virtually inexhaustible. Despite known revolts by subject peoples or satraps, the solidity of the imperial edifice was beyond question; and at that time the Great King, the virtual lieutenant on earth of the supreme god Ahura Mazda, could count absolutely on the loyalty of the Persian aristocracy. So it was an adventure fraught with fearful risk that faced Alexander when he left Macedonia in 334 BC with all of his men, bound first for the Hellespont and then for Asia Minor.

Thirty years after Cyrus's conquests, a series of rebellions in the empire was stamped out by Darius I between 522 and 521 BC. His exploits were recorded on the cliffs at Bisutun, on the road from Babylon to Ecbatana (above and opposite): The Great King has placed his foot on his leading rival, while the other rebellious kings, ropes around their necks, await their turn. Behind Darius are two of the six Persian noblemen who had helped him to power, one depicted as a spear-carrier, the other bearing Darius's bow. The great god Ahura Mazda gazes down upon the scene.

In the spring of 334 the Macedonian army landed on the coast of Asia Minor, near Troy. Alexander immediately made his intentions clear by driving a spear into the soil, a sign that he was laying claim to the Great King's lands. Next he performed a series of symbolic ritual acts deliberately intended to associate himself with the heroes of the Trojan War.

CHAPTER II
CONQUEST OF THE COASTS

Convinced of his military superiority, Alexander raced fearlessly into large-scale action against the Persian Empire (opposite: In hand-to-hand combat early in the campaign), invoking the protection of the semidivine heroes of the Trojan War. Above: Honoring the grave of the Greek hero Achilles.

Alexander's army was of formidable efficiency, and the Macedonians were its moving force and often its decisive component

Alexander had been careful not to leave Macedonia entirely unprotected: 12,000 foot soldiers and 1,500 cavalry remained behind to maintain order under the command of Antipater, a veteran general who had fought under Alexander's father.

His mounted troops, no more than 1,800 in number, were offspring of the noble families of the Macedonian kingdom's diverse regions. They bore the collective name of Companion Cavalry, or simply— the Companions (*hetairoi*). Wearing helmets, they fought chiefly with a short dogwood stabbing-spear which they used to wound and unhorse their enemy.

As for the infantry, recruited from the Macedonian peasantry and 30,000 to 43,000 strong, it fought in phalanx, or wedge, formation, with each soldier wielding a spear nearly 18 feet (5½ meters) long, known as the *sarissa,* which rendered each compact cluster of men virtually impenetrable and indestructible.

In addition to his Macedonians, Alexander had raised 7,000 infantry and 600 cavalry troops from the Greek city-states of the Corinthian League. The famed Thessalian horse soldiers were represented by 1,800 men. The Balkan peoples (Thracians, Paeonians, Illyrians) also sent valuable contingents: light infantry, cavalry, and javelin-throwers.

"Physically he was very beautiful and almost tireless. His intelligence was penetrating, his courage boundless; none loved glory and danger more; none was so attentive to his duties toward the gods. He was the complete master of bodily pleasures, and proved insatiable only for the pleasures of the mind, for the glory they bore him."

Arrian
Campaigns of Alexander,
2d century AD

Above: The profile of Alexander on a Greek coin.

Horsemen and foot-soldiers operated closely together in the Macedonian army. The Companion Cavalry (left, depicted on a gravestone) fought protected by a breastplate and sword, while the infantry carried a long spear and heavy shield (below).

Hundreds of chariots also set out alongside the fighting men in Alexander's quest to conquer Asia Minor

The baggage-train left first, providing transport for food and siege equipment. It was organized under a general with thousands of army servants at his command. There were also the personal entourages of the soldiers, including wives and servants. The Macedonians who had not brought along their wives took concubines in the conquered lands. Entire new households were generated along the line of march: In 325 BC, for example, something like 10,000 babies were born in the Greek camp. In addition the troops were followed by a host of merchants, who were eager to profit from drought or famine. As the soldiers piled up booty, the baggage train grew constantly more bloated. Many of the troops thought less of war and its dangers than they did of amassing wealth.

To command and deploy his troops, Alexander had selected a number of seasoned fighters, most of them of noble stock

Some of Alexander's generals were of his father's generation: Among these were Parmenio, whose political and strategic counsels were often badly received by Alexander, or Antigonus the One-Eyed, who would play a leading part after the young king's death.

Alexander grew to rely increasingly on men of his own age, such as Hephaestion, his companion since childhood and by far the dearest of his friends. Many other young men from the highest ranks of the Macedonian aristocracy were ready to serve the king, including Craterus, Seleucus, Ptolemy, and Perdiccas. These men commanded regiments and battalions of horse and infantry. In 334 the honor of commanding the royal battalion fell to Cleitus, Alexander's own foster brother. The king's closest companions, numbering less than a dozen, bore the coveted title of *somatophylax* (bodyguard). But in every instance the final decisions were made by Alexander, who fought in person at the head of his troops astride his warhorse Bucephalus, and

Like all noble-born Macedonian youths, Alexander (left) was raised to be a great horseman. His tutors had trained him to be a warrior with a toughened body as well as a prince equipped to take over the kingdom.

was identifiable from afar by his helmet with white egret plumes on either side.

Chroniclers assigned to cover the conquest also took part in the expedition

One of the most famous chroniclers was Ptolemy, Alexander's right-hand man and also author of memoirs which are now unfortunately lost. After the king's death Ptolemy was appointed governor of Egypt, where he founded the dynasty of the Ptolemies. The ship's log kept by Alexander's admiral, Nearchus, was fortunately transcribed by the Roman-era historian

Raised among companions of his own age, Alexander naturally chose the same young men to be his advisers and generals. Above: A mosaic from Pella shows Craterus, one of Alexander's companions, hunting a lion.

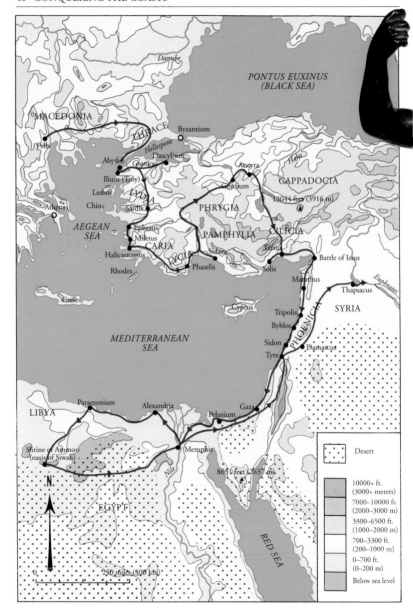

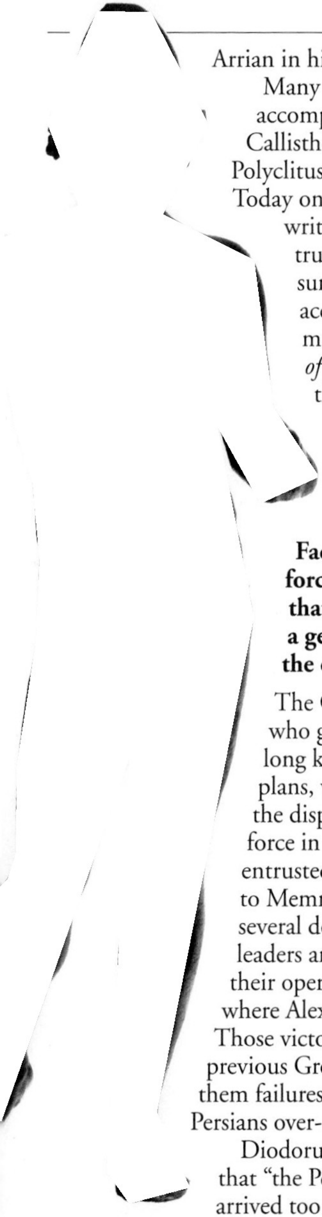

Arrian in his study of India. Many other chroniclers accompanied the conqueror: Callisthenes, Aristotle, Anaximenes, Polyclitus, Aristobulus, and Marsyas. Today only sparse fragments of their writings survive. The same is true for Alexander's military surveyors. But all their accounts served as the base material for countless *Histories of Alexander* written during the Roman era, either in Latin (Quintus Curtius, Justin) or in Greek (Arrian, Diodorus Siculus, Plutarch).

Faced with this threatening force, Darius still did not feel that the situation called for a general mobilization of the empire

The Great King Darius III, who gained the throne in 336, had long known of the Macedonian plans, which were made plain by the dispatch of an expeditionary force in 337. At that time he had entrusted command of his troops to Memnon, who had inflicted several defeats on the Macedonian leaders and forced them to limit their operations to the Trojan plain, where Alexander had now landed. Those victories, and the memory of previous Greek expeditions—all of them failures—had doubtless made the Persians over-confident of their power.

Diodorus tells us, for example, that "the Persian satraps and generals arrived too late to prevent the

The early conquests of Alexander (shown at left in a Roman bronze statue), carried out between 334 and 332 BC, stretched from the Black Sea south to the Nile valley. In early spring 334, he landed close to Troy. At the end of May, thrusting into Hellespontine (coastal) Phrygia, he won the battle of Granicus and flung open the road to Sardis, the center of Persian power in Asia Minor. One by one the great Greek cities of the coast were liberated from the Persians: Ephesus, Priene, Miletus. In the summer he continued his southward march and laid siege to Halicarnassus, the capital of Caria (present-day Bodrum, Turkey). In the autumn he subdued Lycia and Pamphylia before turning north again toward Greater (inland) Phrygia and Gordium, where he established winter quarters. In the spring of 333 he turned south again, seizing Tarsus, capital of Cilicia. In early November, at Issus, he again vanquished Darius and conquered the Phoenician cities of Byblos and Sidon. From January to August 332 he successfully besieged Tyre, before marching south to reach Egypt in the autumn of the year.

Macedonians from crossing," although at the time the Persians could raise a navy of at least 300 vessels—far superior to Alexander's fleet of some 180 ships.

The satraps joined forces at Zeleia, in northern Asia Minor. Two very different strategic concepts were about to collide.

Memnon, originally from the Greek island of Rhodes but long since related to a great Persian family, proposed scorched-earth tactics. He probably knew that Alexander's reserves of cash and foodstuffs were slender: in all, perhaps enough to maintain and feed his army for a month. Like many other conquerors, the Macedonian clearly planned to live off the land, but to do that he needed to achieve a swift victory. To deny him battle and destroy the local source of food would thus have been an intelligent move.

The Persian leaders, however, saw things differently—furthermore, they were hesitant to take

Persian noblemen functioned both as satraps and as generals, entering the fray against Alexander in the front line of battle. Above: A coin with the head of a Persian satrap.

advice from a general of Greek origin. Sure of their superiority in battle, concerned to protect their lands from looting, and eager to announce victory to Darius and thus reap an abundance of fresh honors, they were impatient to face the young prince who had just landed, sword in hand, from Europe.

In May 334 the Persian generals made a move

Hoping to create a strong defensive position that Alexander might be lured into attacking, the Persians grouped their cavalry on the sloping banks of the Granicus River. In doing so, however, they neutralized their ability to

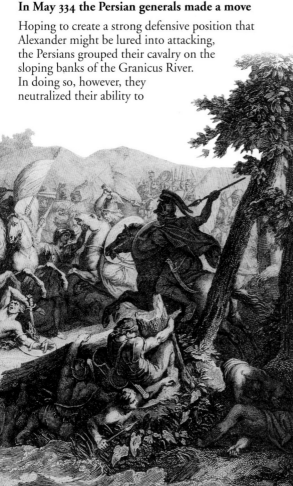

The first major clash between Greeks and Persians took place on the banks of the Granicus River (below), with only small cavalry units from either side taking part in the struggle.

"Standing shoulder to shoulder, the 'Royal Kinsmen' began by hurling their javelins at Alexander. Then, fighting hand to hand, they braved every imaginable danger in their attempts to slay him. But the king refused to be defeated by the multitude of his foes, despite the number and the extent of the perils surrounding him. His breastplate was struck twice, his helmet once, and three strokes fell on the shield he had taken from the Temple of Athena [in Troy]. But far from giving up, he raised his head high against all dangers, glorying in desperate courage. And numberless were the other leaders, famous among the Persians, who fell to the ground not far from him."

Diodorus Siculus
Historical Library,
1st century BC

maneuver. When Alexander led a surprise attack at dawn, the collision of the two masses of cavalry was extremely violent. Alexander himself plunged into the fighting at the head of his men. Several thousand Persian cavalry fled from the battlefield. As for the thousands of Greek mercenaries serving under the Persians, they were slaughtered on the spot. Two thousand survivors were condemned to forced labor in Macedonia's mines.

The victorious Alexander's first priority was to organize the conquered territories

Alexander's constant concern was to preserve the continuity of the Persian—or Achaemenid—dynastic institutions. He left intact the organization of the provinces into satrapies. In Hellespontine Phrygia (whose capital surrendered without a fight), the Macedonian Calas was named satrap, and the population was ordered to pay the same tribute to its new master as it had previously delivered to Darius.

Ephesus in 334 BC was the wealthiest and most famous of the cities of Asia Minor, and a point of contact between the Greek and Persian civilizations. Plutarch reports that on the day Alexander was born the Temple of Artemis (below and opposite) went up in flames.

Soon afterward, Alexander bloodlessly acquired Sardis, the virtual center of Persian hegemony in western Asia Minor. The city, the former capital of the Lydian kings, was strongly fortified. But the Persian Mithrines, doubtless discouraged by the recent disaster at the Granicus River, surrendered both citadel and treasury to Alexander. This is the first known instance of the surrender of a Persian nobleman; from then on Mithrines remained at Alexander's side, enjoying the same honors as under Darius. Alexander was later to develop this Macedonian-Iranian cooperation even further. In both Sardis and Dascylium, the local administrative structures were left in place, although all the major posts (civil, military, and financial) were put exclusively in the hands of Macedonians and Greeks.

"It is no surprise that the temple was burned to ashes, given that at the time Artemis was fully occupied bringing Alexander into the world. All the Magi then at Ephesus, seeing in the temple's destruction the omen of another disaster…cried out that this day had brought forth a scourge and a calamity of great import for Asia.**"**

Hegesias of Magnesia, quoted by Plutarch, in "Life of Alexander," 1st–2d century AD

Through the spring and summer of 334 BC the conqueror snapped up the Greek cities along the coast

Many of the coastal cities chose to ally themselves with the Macedonian king. In fact, some of them—such as Ephesus—had been deserted by their Achaemenid garrisons. At Miletus, however, the Greek commander of the citadel decided to resist, counting both on the city's fortifications and on the expected support of the Persian fleet and army. But Alexander's ships managed to head off the Persian fleet. Cut off by land and sea Miletus was forced to yield.

As a general rule, when Alexander took possession he established democratic government in the cities he had liberated, unlike the Persians, who had installed local tyrants, often loathed by the majority of the population. At Ephesus, the wholesale slaughter of the tyrants and their kin by the inhabitants assumed such proportions that Alexander had to intervene to stop it.

But their liberation from Persian domination did not mean that the cities achieved full independence. They were forced to contribute to the costs of Alexander's expedition, and sometimes their Persian garrisons were replaced by Macedonian ones. Alexander was no longer simply the liberator of the Greek cities: He considered himself successor to the Great King as lord of lands and people. The Greek cities of Asia Minor had no choice but to accept him.

After the loss of Miletus, Memnon and the Persians fell back on Halicarnassus in southwest Asia Minor. The capital of the twin satrapies of Caria and Lycia, Halicarnassus was chiefly known for its Mausoleum— one of the seven wonders of the ancient world—where the great satrap Mausolus was buried. Alexander foresaw a long, drawn-out siege of the city, which possessed powerful fortifications, sappers, and an arsenal of defensive machinery. The Persian leaders, exhausted by sallies and assaults, were forced to abandon the town and take refuge in the citadel, which they held for a full year.

Below: A fragment from the pediment of the Mausoleum at Halicarnassus. Right: Renaissance fresco depicting the episode of the Gordian Knot.

"The knot was tied with thongs of cornel bark, and none could see where it began and where it ended. Although he could find no way of loosing this knot, Alexander refused to leave it intact…; according to some, he therefore cut it in two with a stroke of his sword. But Aristobolus says that he withdrew the dowel-peg which ran through pole, holding the knot together, and thus releasing the thongs."

Arrian
Campaigns of Alexander,
2d century AD

Alexander cuts the Gordian Knot

Leaving a garrison behind in Caria, and sending his main force on to Sardis, Alexander led part of his army on the conquest of the coastal districts of southern Asia Minor before swerving northward to winter at Gordium. At Gordium, according to legend, Alexander proved himself worthy of the title "Lord of all Asia" and fulfilled a prophecy by undoing an impossible knot that had confounded would-be rulers for ages. Rather than skillfully loosening the knot, Alexander simply pulled out his knife and cut it!

Meanwhile, the Persians had mounted a vigorous counterattack on Alexander's rear. Memnon, promoted now to supreme commander of the Asia Minor front and the Persian naval forces, attacked by sea. Taking advantage of the fact that Alexander had sent most of his fleet home, with the exception of transport vessels, Memnon seized the islands of Chios and Lesbos in the spring and summer of 333, with the intention of crossing over to Europe. His offensive action stirred up great hopes in the Cycladic Islands and in several cities on the European shore that had been "liberated" against their will by Alexander. When Memnon died toward the end of the summer, his loss was a blow to the Persian camp, even though his successor, his nephew Pharnabazus, continued to operate successfully in the Aegean Sea. In the meantime Alexander, apparently becoming aware of his mistake, had moved to put back together a fleet assigned to clear the islands of their newly restored Persian garrisons.

In early spring of 333 BC Alexander left Gordium and marched toward the Cilician shore, one of the traditional bases for Persian naval supremacy. At Tarsus, capital of the region, he fell seriously ill, probably as a result of hypothermia contracted during a swim in the icy Cydnus River. His progress was halted for several weeks. But thanks to the care of his physician he recovered and resumed his march on Syria.

On Persian coins (left) the Great King was often depicted as an archer, symbolizing his role as a warrior.

Below: A dagger from the Achaemenid dynasty.

The archers of the royal guard were known as the Immortals because, according to Herodotus, as soon as one fell in battle another of the same stature at once replaced him. Wielding a long spear, they bore bow and quivers on their backs (left).

"Immediately behind them came those the Persians called the Immortals, some ten thousand men. These were made the more imposing by adornment of barbarian opulence: for them gold collars, for them gold-brocaded robes and long-sleeved tunics studded with gems."
Quintus Curtius
History of Alexander,
1st century AD

To counter the Macedonian advance, Darius in person assumed command of the royal armies

The makeup of this new Persian force was very different from the army that had opposed Alexander a year earlier. All the peoples of the empire were expected to contribute their contingents, with the exception of the populations of the Iranian plateau and India, whose troops would have taken too long to mobilize. The army gathered near Babylon in an almost numberless throng of horsemen and foot soldiers.

Indeed their exact numbers are difficult to estimate. The Roman historian Quintus Curtius gives a total of

316,200 men, while other authors of antiquity go as far as 600,000. In fact, the number of actual fighting men must be reduced to tens of thousands, for the royal army contained a high proportion of non-combatants. Babylonian records, for example, indicate that each horseman was accompanied by twelve servants! Moreover, when the Great King assumed command of the army it meant that the whole court embarked on what amounted to a mass migration: Wives and children of the royal family and of high dignitaries, administrators, officers, and above all servants of every kind, were set into motion by the thousands. Darius would leave the bulk of this entourage behind at Damascus just before the battle, and shortly afterward Parmenio would capture no fewer than 778 persons attached to the person of the Great King, including 319 kitchen workers and 329 concubines, all of them skilled musicians.

Descriptions of the booty taken at Damascus give a startling idea of the extent of the royal treasury that lay strewn on the ground: silver earmarked for enormous payments to the army, vestments of a host of noble men and women, gold place settings, golden horse-bits, tents decorated with royal splendor, and chariots abandoned by their owners and overflowing with unheard-of wealth.

The first pitched battle of the two royal armies took place in November 333 in Cilicia, near the town of Issus

It was a particularly unfortunate choice of battlefield, for the Persian army and cavalry had no chance of deploying freely across a narrow plain hemmed in by mountains and sea. Despite the fire and bravery of his cavalry—the pride and joy of the Great King—the superior maneuverability of the Macedonian forces once more won the day. Once it became clear that disaster was imminent, Darius chose to flee the battlefield rather than fall into the hands of his foe. But the defeat did not

Facing Alexander in person on the battlefield for the first time, Darius fought from his war-chariot, surrounded by the spearmen of his guard (opposite).

"Alexander turned his gaze in all directions, seeking Darius. As soon as he saw him, he raced into the field with his horsemen, straight for the Great King in person, for more than achieving victory over the Persians he wished to be the personal instrument of victory."

Diodorus Siculus
Historical Library,
1st century BC

The most famous ancient representation of Alexander and Darius in battle is this celebrated Roman mosaic, a copy of a Greek painting, of the battle of Issus, found in the House of the Faun at Pompeii.

Far left: Alexander; near left: The dismayed Persians flee the field.

mean the end of Persian resistance. Darius still possessed enormous reserves of men and money, and some of his surviving generals even mounted a counter-offensive in Asia Minor. But the road to Phoenicia now lay open before Alexander.

The Great King's defeat and flight were particularly damaging politically

The man who on his public monuments styled himself the greatest cavalryman, archer, and spearman had not merely been defeated: He had run away, leaving behind him the insignia of power, his royal cloak, his bow, and

"The king took with him one of his friends, Hephaestion, and they went to greet the [captive] women. Both men wore identical clothing, and Hephaestion was both taller and more handsome. Sysigambis therefore took Hephaestion for the king and prostrated herself before him."

his chariot. From that day on, Macedonian historians would tirelessly repeat this story in order to discredit Darius who, it was claimed, had thereby lost all legitimacy, particularly when compared to Alexander's striking physical courage. The same propaganda presented the Macedonian king as a model of loftiness of soul. Indeed, in his haste to flee, Darius had abandoned his mother, Sisygambis, his wife Stateira, two of his daughters, and his young son. The victor treated these prisoners with respect—yet another way of presenting himself as the legitimate successor to Darius, whose preliminary peace overtures he contemptuously rejected.

"Then, disconcerted by her mistake, she turned to bow to Alexander. But the king spoke and said, 'Fear nothing, Mother: he too is Alexander.' By thus calling the old woman Mother he gave a taste of the kindness with which these women would be treated."

Diodorus Siculus
Historical Library,
1st century BC

"And henceforth when you have occasion to address me, do so as to the king of Asia: do not write as equal to equal"

With those words, written in response to Darius's peace overtures, Alexander marched into Phoenicia, the most important Achaemenid naval base. Sidon surrendered without a fight, but Tyre refused to allow Alexander to enter the shrine of Melkart, thus stressing its determination to remain free. Located on an island, the city presented great problems to its attackers at a time (February 332) when the Persians were still supreme at sea. At the cost of heavy casualties, Alexander managed to build a causeway linking the mainland to the island. Then he summoned engineers from Cyprus and the length and breadth of Phoenicia to build siege towers, some erected on the causeway, others floated on cavalry-transport vessels.

The Tyrians put up a tenacious defense, using every known tactic to break the siege: They attempted to set the enemy ships on fire with flaming arrows, to smash them by hurling enormous blocks of stone from the battlements. They even sent underwater swimmers to cut their anchor-cables.

Fortunately for Alexander, other Phoenician cities (Byblos and Aradus), as well as Rhodes and the cities of Cyprus, rallied to him. Hemmed in behind their walls, the Tyreans turned back a series of assaults before yielding in August 332. It was a major victory for Alexander, since he now had superiority at sea, as well as on land.

Phoenician ports supplied the Persian Empire with the bulk of its war fleet and seamen. Tyre was the wealthiest and most powerful of them—hence Alexander's relentless siege of the city (above), which lasted ten months. Left: Detail of a siege engine.

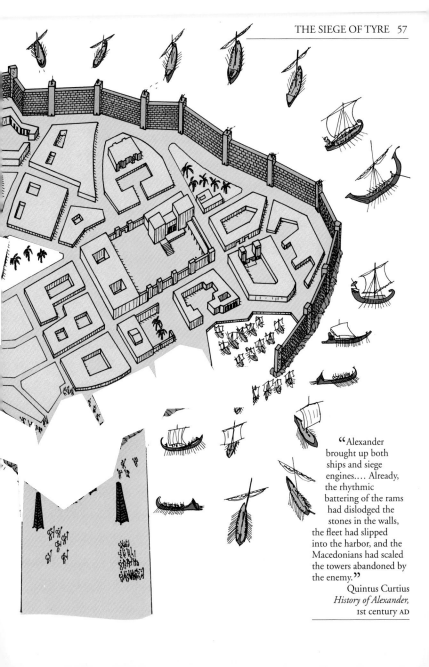

"Alexander brought up both ships and siege engines.... Already, the rhythmic battering of the rams had dislodged the stones in the walls, the fleet had slipped into the harbor, and the Macedonians had scaled the towers abandoned by the enemy."
Quintus Curtius
History of Alexander,
1st century AD

Nothing now stood between the victorious Alexander and the road to Egypt

Only Gaza, strongly fortified and defended by Persian and Arab units under the command of Batis, offered a short-lived resistance. In the autumn of 332 Alexander made his entrance into Egypt at Pelusium. Meeting no resistance from the Persian satrap Mazaces, he took possession of Memphis, the capital. The Egyptians readily accepted the new conqueror, who, like his Persian predecessors, made a point of sacrificing to the local gods, showing particular respect to the sacred bull Apis, the living incarnation of the god Ptah. This victory on land went hand in hand with complete seaborne success, for the Macedonian fleet had by now succeeded in sweeping the Persians from the Aegean. To mark his possession of the Egyptian shore, Alexander founded a new city in the Nile Delta, which he named after himself: Alexandria, the future capital of Ptolomaic Egypt.

He also decided to consult the oracle of Ammon, a westward trek of several weeks into the desert oasis at Siwah. By good fortune, his march was studded with a whole series of divine signs: Zeus decreed life-giving rain, and a flock of crows guided the little group when it was lost amid the sands. Entering the shrine, Alexander questioned the priest about his fate. This was a most formative event in Alexander's life. Although no one ever learned the response, he told his friends afterwards that he had heard what his heart desired. It is often speculated that he sought to discover if he was, in fact, the son of a god, and whether he would be successful in the conquest of Asia.

When he left Alexandria, he left power theoretically in the hands of an Egyptian governor, but real military and economic control lay in Greek and Macedonian hands.

Coins spread the image of the hero-king far and wide. Below: The young conqueror wears the ram's horns of the Egyptian god Ammon, who, it was said, promised him

mastery of the world at the Siwah oasis.

Entering Egypt in triumph, Alexander was welcomed by the local aristocracy. He also sought harmonious relations with the priests, privileged pillars of pharaonic power. At Luxor the sanctuary was modified to become a chapel on whose walls Alexander (opposite, shown at left) is depicted as pharaoh, facing the god Min, to whom he pays homage.

For three years Alexander went from conquest to conquest. He had led his men for thousands of miles and forced scores of cities and states into submission, but he had never utterly defeated Darius. After the disaster at Issus, the Great King marshaled a new army at Babylon. In the spring of 331 the Macedonians set out once again for Mesopotamia.

CHAPTER III
THE PILLARS OF EMPIRE CRUMBLE

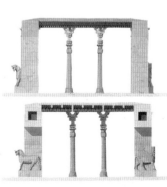

In a few victorious months, in the autumn and winter of 331–30, Alexander seized the Great King's palaces at Babylon, Susa, Persepolis, and Pasargadae. Opposite: Making a triumphant entry. Right: Architectural details from Persepolis.

This time Darius sent out a call for every available man, bringing them in from the farthest corners of the empire. According to some ancient chroniclers, he mustered between 500,000 and a million troops—although Quintus Curtius's estimate of 200,000 infantry and 45,000 cavalry seems more likely. Among them were the renowned Bactrian horsemen and armored Scythian warriors from the steppes of Central Asia. Two hundred scythed chariots would constitute the spearhead of the army. Quintus Curtius wrote: "Iron-pointed spears protruded ahead of the horses; three sword-blades were affixed on either side of the yoke; javelin points stuck outward from the spokes of the wheels; scythe blades welded to the wheel rims mowed down everything the horses encountered in their charge."

"[At Gaugamela, seen below] the Macedonians began to surround the chariots and pick off their crews. The immense disaster had strewn the front line with horses and charioteers, who were no longer able to control their frenzied steeds, whose wild head-tossing had shaken loose their traces and even overturned the chariots. The wounded horses dragged the dead behind them. Their terror prevented them from stopping, their exhaustion from going forward.…"

The Great King made camp near the village of Gaugamela on the Royal Road

Mindful of the lessons of Issus, Darius selected a wide plain ideal for cavalry maneuvers: He even had the plain leveled, and ordered his men to embed iron spikes in the ground to wound the enemy horses.

By now (early in July 331) Alexander had marched up from Tyre and reached the Euphrates at Thapsacus. The man ordered to block Alexander's way, the satrap Mazaeus of Babylon, had withdrawn from the left bank of the river, and Alexander was able to take his men across on two bridges constructed by his engineers. Surprisingly, the Persians also failed to oppose his crossing of the Tigris River.

Battle was joined on 1 October. The scythed chariots

"...Meanwhile a small group of four-horse chariots managed to push through to the rear ranks, killing those on its path: amputated limbs lay everywhere, and since the still-hot wounds as yet caused no pain, the soldiers, despite mutilation and exhaustion, held on to their weapons until the instant they dropped dead."

Quintus Curtius
History of Alexander,
1st century AD

failed to be as effective as Darius had hoped, for Alexander had instructed his men to pull aside as the vehicles approached and then riddle the charioteers with arrows. Despite a heroic charge by Mazaeus on the Persian right wing, defeat was once more in store for the Persians. Again Darius fled, leaving in Alexander's hands treasure worth roughly 4,000 talents (between 75 and 100 tons of silver), his bow, his arrows, and his chariot.

Instead of pursuing Darius, Alexander headed for Babylon

A renowned and ancient city, strongly fortified, Babylon had been embellished by the succeeding dynasties that ruled from it. Capital of the satrapy of Babylonia ever since Cyrus the Great, it was also one of the Great King's residences, site of one of Darius's palaces. Lying at the heart of a region made arable by irrigation, Babylon was a very wealthy city, as were its famous religious shrines, which were run like great estates by administrators drawn from the local aristocracy. Instead of resisting, Mazaeus rode out with his sons to meet Alexander, escorted by the city's civil and religious leaders. This move, and the presentation of rich gifts, were clearly a token of unconditional surrender.

The battlefield of Gaugamela was a vast scrimmage (opposite), as imagined by the Flemish painter Jan Brueghel the Younger, or a more orderly confrontation, as depicted by the 4th-century BC Greek vase painter (below): Both scenes represent the moment when Darius's fate was sealed. Alexander, on horseback, and the Great King, in his chariot, clash in symbolic combat. With victory slipping away, Darius—as he had done at Issus—fled the field.

"The Macedonian soldiers heard the slapping of the reins with which the charioteer belabored the royal steeds: It was the only trace Darius left in his headlong flight."
Quintus Curtius
History of Alexander,
1st century AD

Alexander made his official and triumphant entrance into the city aboard a chariot, riding through streets strewn with flowers and crowns and lined with silver altars; he took possession of the palace and the citadel, while the Persian ruler handed him the keys to the treasury. As in Egypt Alexander was careful to display public respect for the Babylonian shrines, offering up a sacrifice to Bel Marduk, the greatest of the Babylonian gods.

Alexander re-appointed Mazaeus as satrap of Babylon; Mithrines, the former head of the garrison at Sardis, became satrap of Armenia. These administrative appointments marked a turning-point in Alexander's policy, for they were the first time that he elevated Persians to such high posts. Naturally, though, it was to Greeks and Macedonians that Alexander entrusted the military and fiscal control of his growing empire. Nonetheless his appointment of Mazaeus meant that a certain number of Persians came over to Alexander's side; it also demonstrated the king's determination to give them responsible positions in the empire he was conquering—and recreating in the Achaemenid mold.

At the end of September, Susa surrendered, just as Babylon had done. Oxathres, son of the satrap Abulites, came out to greet the king, who entered the city with great ceremony at the head of the satrap's gifts—dromedaries and elephants from India. Abulites continued to rule as satrap.

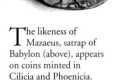

Built on the banks of the Choaspes, Susa seemed to the Greeks the pinnacle of Achaemenid capitals

Herodotus considered Susa the end of the Royal Road from Sardis. Apart from the palaces built there by various kings, it boasted one of the empire's largest treasure-stores, where the Great Kings stocked their precious metals.

The likeness of Mazaeus, satrap of Babylon (above), appears on coins minted in Cilicia and Phoenicia.

Right: Bust of Alexander by Lysippus

SIC VIRTVS EVENIT.

The ancient authors estimated its value at between 40,000 and 50,000 talents—from 1,000 to 1,250 tons of gold—plus 9,000 talents (225 tons) of the gold coins known as *darics*.

Alexander, who had already laid hands on the treasure of several satrapies and the treasure-stores of Babylonia, now possessed substantial reserves of precious metals. He had left his initial financial difficulties far behind him. At the conqueror's instructions, part of the treasure was to be melted down for coin in Babylonian workshops, with the *daric* remaining the royal currency.

After his victory at Gaugamela, Alexander rode in triumph into Babylon, a scene imagined above in a 17th-century French tapestry.

"Alexander's appearance is best captured in the statues executed by Lysippus—who was also the only sculptor whose portraits the king himself prized."

Plutarch
"Life of Alexander,"
1st–2d century AD

Now backed by inexhaustible reserves, Alexander considered raising fresh troops in Europe

The ancient authors play down the casualties suffered by the Macedonians in these battles, putting them at 85 cavalry for Granicus, 100 for Gaugamela. They attribute much heavier losses to the Persian forces: 1,000 cavalry at Granicus, 100,000 killed at Issus (including 10,000 horse), and 300,000 enemy bodies counted at Gaugamela. These figures should be viewed with caution, particularly when account is taken of those wounded—many of them fatally—and of soldiers

Embellished by Darius I late in the 6th century BC, Susa was the former capital of the kings of Elam. An immense palace was built there, decorated by Babylonian artists drawing on Assyrian art. The 4th-century winged sphinxes above served as guardian spirits protecting the outer palace walls.

exhausted by forced marches at the height of summer between Tyre and the valley of the Tigris. Moreover, Alexander left many large units behind him to occupy conquered territory and complete the subjugation of the enemy. He was thus in constant need of reinforcements. In the autumn of 334 he sent all newly married soldiers back to Macedonia and ordered his lieutenants to raise every man in the country for the infantry and cavalry. In the autumn of 332 he dispatched Amyntas from Gaza to Macedonia with orders to select young candidates for military service. Macedonian reinforcements and Greek mercenaries had already reached him at Gordium (3,350 men) and Tyre (4,000 mercenaries). Amyntas

The Sacred Way of Babylon began at the Ishtar Gate (below), decorated with blue glazed brick set with relief images of real and mythical animals: 575 dragons and bulls and 120 lions.

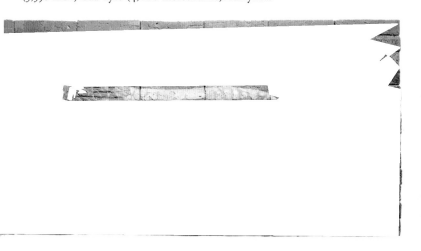

now brought back with him, either to Babylon or Susa, fresh troops consisting of 6,500 Macedonians, 4,100 Thracians, and 4,380 Greek mercenaries. At Babylon Menes, his appointee as satrap of Syria, also received funds for the purpose of recruiting as many mercenaries as possible.

The contribution of the western Greek states was particularly noteworthy in view of opposition in Greece to Macedonian rule. Revolt broke out first of all in Thrace—led by the Macedonian general left there to run the country. Next, Sparta took the lead in a rebellion,

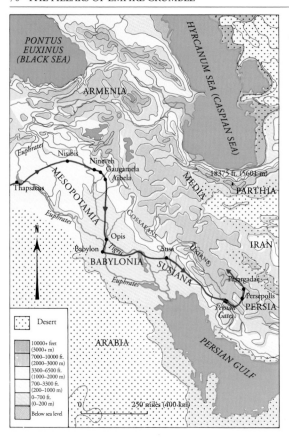

Following the battle of Gaugamela, in early October 331, Alexander took the Royal Road to Babylon, passing through inhabited regions rich in supplies. From Babylon he crossed the Tigris and pushed eastward, reaching Susa in ten days. Soon his route turned north towards Persia. While the main body of the army moved to Persepolis through the pass of the Persian Gates, Alexander took a small detachment into the mountains, where he stormed the positions of one of Darius's lieutenants at the Persian Gates. In January 330 he entered Persepolis. The following winter he took Pasargadae.

"A triple wall encircled [the citadel at Persepolis, opposite]. Seven cubits in height [about ten feet; three meters], the outer wall was set with guardposts in the form of towers; the middle wall was twice as high. The third or inner wall was made of hard stone strong enough to endure forever."
Diodorus Siculus
Historical Library,
1st century BC

even managing to score an early victory against a Macedonian army. But this was eventually in vain, for Sparta was now in irreversible decline. Not until October 331 did Antipater succeed in putting an end to the tumult, and allay the anxieties of Alexander, who was fully occupied in Babylonia.

The reinforced army now headed for Persia, its goal: Persepolis

After the fearful heat of the Babylonian summer, the warriors from Europe encountered cold and snow on

the Iranian plateau. The great highway from Susa to
Persepolis was guarded by a sequence of fortresses.
Madates, a blood relative of Darius, commanded the first
of them. Alexander handed over the bulk of his forces to
Parmenio, ordering him to make for Persepolis along the
great highway leading through Kazerun and Shiraz.
While he and the remaining troops thrust into the hills
to smoke out a Persian army of between 20,000 and
40,000 foot soldiers and 700 horsemen, guarding the
pass known as the Persian Gates. There he collided with
the Uxian people, whose leaders received annual gifts
from the Great King as a means of sealing their alliance.
After mounting a bloody raid against them, Alexander
imposed a yearly tribute of 100 horses, 500 beasts of
burden, and 30,000 sheep.

Unable to pierce the Persian defenses at the pass,
Alexander led his force along a goat-trail and came down
into the valley behind the Persians. He then crossed
the Araxes (Pulvar) River, and arrived at Persepolis in
January 330. He made his entrance without meeting
any resistance—as the Persian governor, Tiridates, had
promised in a letter. Politically speaking, it was a victory
of major significance.

Persepolis, built at Darius II's command, and embellished by all his successors, was the empire's historic—and most famous—capital

The palaces, storehouses, and treasury of Persepolis, as
well as its ornate architecture and statuary, symbolized
and exalted the person of the king and Persian mastery
over all the peoples of the empire.

Fabulous booty awaited Alexander's soldiers; according
to Diodorus Siculus, "The Macedonians poured into the
city, slaughtering all the men and ransacking the houses.
They found silver in abundance, and gold for the taking;
a great store of rich vestments, some embroidered in
purple, some in cloth of gold, fell into the victors'
hands. They pillaged all day long without slaking their
insatiable greed. As for the women, all laden with
jewelry, they dragged them off by force, treating the
throng of female war prisoners as slaves." Alexander
himself took possession of the enormous royal treasury—

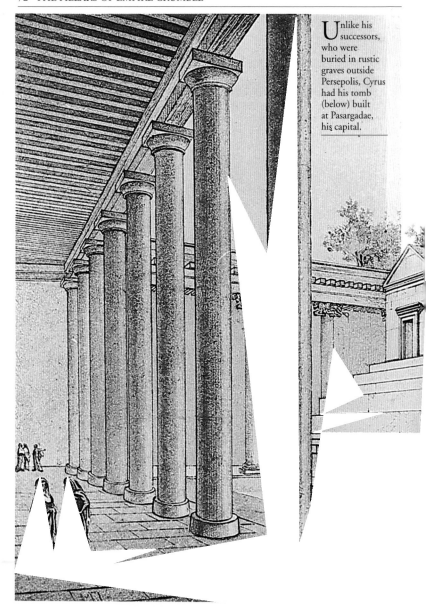

Unlike his successors, who were buried in rustic graves outside Persepolis, Cyrus had his tomb (below) built at Pasargadae, his capital.

120,000 talents, or 3,000 tons of gold—and decided to transfer a large part of it to Susa. According to Plutarch, 10,000 spans of mules and 5,000 camels were barely sufficient to transport the treasure.

After Persepolis, Alexander laid siege to Pasargadae, the former capital of Persia

About twenty-five miles (forty kilometers) north of Persepolis, the city was built by Cyrus following his victory over the Medes, and housed his tomb. It was also at Pasargadae, in a temple dedicated to the goddess Anahita, that the Great Kings were crowned. During the winter of 331–30 Alexander pushed into the depths of Persia, taking possession of the city delivered to him by its governor, and adding the 6,000 talents in its treasury

"Inside this chamber was a sarcophagus of gold in which Cyrus lay buried. Beside it was a bed with golden feet; the bed-linen was of Babylonian weave and the mattress of purple bedclothes. Covering it were a Persian robe and tunics also of Babylonian make."

Arrian
Campaigns of Alexander,
2d century AD

to his financial reserves. He showed particular tact at Cyrus's tomb, so much so that he was nicknamed *philokuros*—"friend of Cyrus." This behavior had a political objective: to show the Persian populations that he respected the royal Achaemenid traditions and to persuade the nobility to join him.

Some Persians were already convinced of the need to collaborate with the conqueror: At Persepolis, for example, Tiridates kept his rank as treasurer, and the satrap appointed by Alexander was a Persian. But this was far from being the general rule. Most

Standing on a hill overlooking a wide plain, Persepolis was a city built from scratch by Darius I. Work on it continued until the last rulers of the dynasty, with each king adding new buildings or transforming existing ones.

Persians remained hostile to Alexander. In their eyes, the "usurper" could neither pass himself off as an Achaemenid nor claim the protection of Persia's great god Ahura Mazda.

Once he returned to Persepolis, the king drew the appropriate conclusions from this failure. In the course of a drinking bout, he set fire to the royal palaces. In a sense, this destructive act marked the end of the Greek war of revenge against the Persian Empire. But it was directed less at pleasing the Greeks than at the Persians themselves: Alexander was determined to show them that the empire they had built was no more, and that he was their new master.

The palace facades (below, a reconstruction of Darius I's residence) were faced with glazed bricks whose colors reflected splendor on the capital. Above a frieze of royal guards, the image of the great god Ahura Mazda is represented by a figure depicted on a winged disk. The palace was set in a garden—the gardens of Persia were fabled—whose luxuriant vegetation softened the hard lines of the building.

After his defeat at Gaugamela, Darius sought refuge at Ecbatana, the summer residence of the Great Kings. There, amid temples and sumptuous palaces adorned with gold and silver leaf, he dreamed of revenge. He was determined to meet Alexander in pitched battle once again, for the last time—and this time the fortunes of war would smile on him.

CHAPTER IV
THE NEW GREAT KING

Persian writers of the Islamic period looked to Alexander as the model of a chivalrous king, just and imbued with the values of Islam. Out of this ideal came a host of images that transformed him into a Muslim prophet (right). It was a marked change from the attitude of pre-Islamic chroniclers, who presented him as a bloodthirsty, destructive conqueror (opposite).

Despite the loss of Babylon, Susa, and Persepolis, Darius still boasted enormous financial reserves. He therefore set about rebuilding a new army around the units that had accompanied him in his flight, and this time he also called on the satrapies lying to the east of Iran. He was not alone at Ecbatana: Barsaentes, satrap of Arachosia, Satibarzanes, satrap of Aria, Bessus, satrap of Bactria, and other noble Persians, including Nabarzanes the Chiliarch (or Grand Vizier), the most important officer of the court, had all remained loyal to Darius. However, confronted with the reluctance of nearby populations to send him troops, he was forced to take flight yet again, heading east with 3,000 cavalry and between 10,000 and 30,000 foot soldiers—after removing 7,000 or 8,000 gold talents (175 or 200 tons) from the treasury at Ecbatana.

Alexander's goal was clear: to seize Darius and put an end to Achaemenid power

Learning from Bisthanes (a nephew of the former Persian king Artaxerxes III) of his enemy's flight, Alexander sent Parmenio and the baggage-train (including all his treasures) to Ecbatana, while he himself set off in a series of forced marches in pursuit of Darius: "Along the line of march such was his haste," wrote Arrian, "that many soldiers were left behind, exhausted, and many horses died. Nevertheless he pressed on at full speed."

Darius continued his eastward march, beyond the Caspian Gates. But this breakneck flight stirred doubts among his followers: The only way to escape the Macedonian pursuer would be to leave the women and baggage on the spot and press on at top speed for eastern Iran. This time the Great King's prestige was at stake. Entire units lost heart and deserted him, and Persians from his entourage left to offer their services to Alexander.

Ecbatana was linked to Bactria by a major strategic highway, garrisoned and lined with caravanserais and sources of water. It crossed mountains through passes that provided natural defenses by slowing the progress of a hostile army. Such, for example, was the purpose of the pass known as the Cilician Gates between Cappadocia and Tarsus, and the Caspian Gates (left) east of Ecbatana, which Darius had just crossed with the aim of forming a new defensive line in Bactria. Alexander passed through without meeting resistance.

Persian chieftains (opposite) carried short straight swords and curved daggers. Even when wearing court dress, Persian noblemen were never without their bows and quivers, from which a whip dangled.

From now on, Darius's greatest danger came from his own people, as a plot was hatched to eliminate him

At the heart of the plot against Darius was the satrap Bessus, who claimed kinship with the Achaemenid family. Supported by Barsaentes and Nabarzanes, and with his own regiments backing him, Bessus ordered Darius's arrest.

The plotters decided that if they learned that Alexander still pursued them, they would hand Darius over, and thus ensure Alexander's favor; if on the contrary they heard that he had turned back, they themselves would then muster the greatest army they could and unite to hold on to their power. To begin with, Bessus himself would command. In July 330, on the news of Alexander's approach, they decided to execute Darius, who had been locked up inside a horse-drawn cart. Barsaentes and Satibarzanes delivered the fatal blows before fleeing.

For Alexander, Darius's murder was a great political windfall

After Darius's death Alexander portrayed himself as the Great King's avenger—rather than usurper. Indeed, later tradition

Below: Darius dying in Alexander's arms.

"After his death he received from Alexander a royal burial, while his children received the same care and upbringing as if he had reigned. And he had Alexander for a son-in-law."

Arrian
Campaigns of Alexander,
2d century AD

In his *Campaigns of Alexander*, Arrian, a 2d-century AD historian, characterized Darius as the typically soft and cowardly barbarian dear to the Greek imagination, thus unwittingly minimizing the extent of Alexander's achievements.

"Such was Darius's end.... He was weak and of poor judgment in matters of war, but for the rest he was never cruel, unless he simply never had occasion to demonstrate cruelty.... His life was an unbroken succession of misfortunes. ... At the very outset, his satraps were defeated at the battle of the Granicus ...then came his own defeat at Issus, where he saw his mother, wife, and children seized as prisoners of war. Moreover, he himself at Arbela [Gaugamela] had dishonored himself by being among the first to flee, and had caused the loss of the greatest army of all the Barbarian race. Then, a wanderer banished from his own empire, he fell victim to the foulest treachery at the hands of his own people, who shut him up in an ignominious carriage, at once king and fettered prisoner; and finally, he perished beneath the blows of his closest intimates joined in conspiracy against him.**"**

Arrian
Campaigns of Alexander,
2d century AD

claimed that Darius had acknowledged Alexander as his heir. The eastward drive against Bessus could be presented as a war waged in the name of Achaemenid ideals: Bessus was not only a regicide but a usurper, for upon his return to Bactria he proclaimed himself Great King.

Moreover, Alexander handled Darius's body with great respect, bearing it with him to Persepolis to be buried in traditional Persian style. Meanwhile, the disappearance of Darius had led the Persian nobles of his entourage to go over in a body to Alexander.

The cooperation of the Iranian ruling class was now vital, as many of Alexander's own units were showing signs of impatience. From Media, the Thessalian and allied Greek cavalry (numbering 7,000 in 334) were sent home, with a handful of 130 Thessalians staying on as mercenaries. This departure marked the end of the Hellenic war of "reprisal," but it risked causing problems for Alexander, who still desperately needed manpower. Simply to guard the treasury at Ecbatana, he had been obliged to leave 6,000 Macedonians in the city.

With Darius dead, the Macedonian soldiers considered that the game was over; they longed to return home

Quintus Curtius reports that a rumor swept the army in Parthia to the effect that "the king, content with what he had achieved, had decided on an immediate return to Macedonia." The soldiers even began to pack their belongings. Alexander was forced to rouse them and delivered an energetic harangue, whose words reputedly inspired the liveliest enthusiasm among the soldiers. Nevertheless, Alexander was postponing rather than settling the problem. In the years ahead the call for locally raised troops was to become a vital necessity, even though reinforcements from Greece and Asia Minor would periodically join him all the way to India.

At the height of summer in 330 BC, Alexander headed directly west for Bactria

He took the great strategic and commercial highway known in the Middle Ages as the Khorassan Road. In agreement with Bessus, Satibarzanes (who had retained his rank of satrap of Aria) rebelled, forcing Alexander to turn south in order to crush the revolt. This caused him to change his overall direction. He now had to approach Bactria by a much longer and more difficult route, crossing Aria, Drangiana, and Arachosia, regions that constitute much of modern-day Afghanistan.

Learning that Satibarzanes had once again risen in revolt in his rear, Alexander dispatched a punitive force to Aria. The resulting pitched battle proved indecisive, and Satibarzanes "issued a challenge to whomever might wish to face him man to man; he himself would fight

In the spring of 330 Alexander set out on the road to Ecbatana to lay hands on Darius, when he learned that Darius had already been assassinated. Alexander, now the new Great King, turned south, toward Aria and the central Iranian plateau, to fight off a rebellion. At the end of the year he took Drangiana, then wintered on the site of present-day Kandahar. Early in the spring of 329 he marched on Bactria (the region around modern Kabul). From Bactria, a land of fertile plains, the troops moved up into the snow- and ice-bound Hindu Kush Mountains. After a brief halt, Alexander crossed the Oxus (modern Amu Darya) River and pushed into Sogdiana (its capital, Maracanda, is the modern Samarkand). Then he marched on to the Jaxartes (modern Syr Darya) River. For the next two years he beat down the resistance of the petty princes of Sogdiana and Bactria. In late spring 327 he again negotiated the Hindu Kush, put his army into training on the site of Alexandria-of-the-Caucasus, and in the autumn led it toward the Indus River.

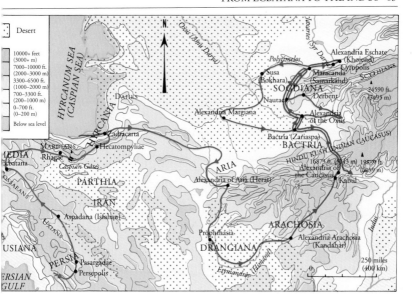

barheaded." A Macedonian chieftain, Erigyius, accepted the challenge. According to Quintus Curtius, "The barbarian was the first to hurl his spear; Erigyius dodged it with a slight sideways motion of his head; then, spurring his horse, he thrust his javelin at the barbarian, the spearpoint piercing his throat and emerging at the back of the neck."

As for the satrap of Arachosia, Barsaentes, Alexander put him to death for his part in Darius's murder.

In the autumn of 330, in the capital of Drangiana, the first open crisis flared between the king and the Macedonian nobility. A quarrel over ceremony ignited the flames

Philotas, one of Alexander's closest friends and the son of his old adviser Parmenio, was accused of treason, arrested, tried, condemned, and executed.

What had happened? The official explanation was that Philotas had been privately critical of Alexander, who had begun to adopt the customs of the Persian

On the banks of the Syr Darya the king founded Alexandria

Eschate (Alexandria-the-Furthest), marking the northernmost boundary of his conquests. Above: a golden medallion embossed with the profile of Alexander.

court, placing a crown on his head, wearing lavish ceremonial robes very similar to those of the Great King, and even using Darius's seal for his correspondence. Further mimicking Persian rulers, he surrounded himself with a harem of 365 concubines. The Macedonians reacted angrily to these actions, even though some of them, such as Hephaestion, chose to side with the king.

In fact Alexander appears to have used the report of a plot against him as a pretext for eliminating a man who had grown too powerful. Once again the troubled history of relations between Macedonian nobility and monarchy rose to the surface. Philotas, general of the Companions, bore the rank of *hipparch,* or commander of cavalry, and was one of the leaders of the nobility. Moreover, his father, Parmenio, would shortly thereafter be murdered by assassins sent to Ecbatana on Alexander's orders.

The violent climax of the affair shows that the king feared the growth of opposition to his authority and policy. Lending greater weight to his fears was the risk that the resentments of the nobility might find an echo among disgruntled army units. To forestall this danger he grouped into a single unit—the Disciplinary Battalion—all those who were angered by Parmenio's death and had spoken against the king, as well as those who in their letters to Macedonia had written things contrary to the king's interests. Alexander was determined that the misplaced frankness of their language should not corrupt the rest of the army.

In spite of hunger, cold, exhaustion, and despair, in the spring of 329 the army resumed its march against Bessus

Alexander's soldiers had to scale the steep slopes of the Hindu Kush Mountains, through the Panshir Valley, under the harshest of conditions. When food supplies ran out they even had to slaughter their beasts of burden; honey, sesame syrup, and wine, all basic staples, fetched astronomical prices, for the local peasants hid their surplus crops in undetectable underground caches.

Bessus himself implemented a scorched-earth policy.

The Persian miniature (opposite), illustrating an epic poem by the 17th-century writer Nizami, shows Alexander canopied and throned in majesty. The poet makes unmistakable references to the Macedonian king's adoption of Achaemenid court customs.

"The customs of his own land, the healthy moderation of Macedonian royal power, seemed to him inadequate to his greatness, and he seized upon the model of Persian monarchy.… He wished ardently to see the conquerors of so many nations gradually stoop to servile functions, sink to the level of captives. Naturally, he said he was merely taking over the abandoned role of the Persians, but by the same token he had adopted their customs, and arrogance of costume led pride of heart in its train."

Quintus Curtius
History of Alexander,
1st century AD

However, taken unawares by Alexander's swift advance, he decided to abandon Bactria and withdraw beyond the Oxus River —whereupon most of his troops deserted him. Without much difficulty, Alexander seized the capital, Bactria, situated in a magnificent oasis, and appointed as satrap a Persian, Artabazes.

Bessus's resistance was short-lived. In a last desperate attempt to block Alexander's path, he ordered the destruction of every bridge and ferry across the Oxus. Nevertheless, the Macedonian soldiers got across by using rafts of animal hides stuffed with straw. Bessus's ambitions were finally cut short through the treachery of a Sogdian nobleman, Spitamenes, and he was handed over to Alexander. Spitamenes himself assumed leadership of the anti-Macedonian struggle. Tortured in "the Persian manner," Bessus had his nose and ears cut off. Then he was tried at Ecbatana by an assembly of Median and Persian nobles and later executed. Darius's murder was thus avenged.

Exactly like Alexander's soldiers, modern Afghan farmers (above) cross the Oxus River on rafts of straw-stuffed hides, which they steer with a pole.

On orders from Alexander, the soldiers put the men to death and took possession of women, children, and any lootable goods

A cycle of rebellion and repression began. The eastward advance became more and more difficult. For two years—329 and 328—Alexander battered at the resistance of the inhabitants of Bactria and above all of Sogdiana. The first rebellion broke out when the king was at Maracanda (modern Samarkand). Trusting to the powerful fortifications of their cities, where the peasants from the countryside had taken shelter, the peoples along the banks of the Jaxartes River rose in revolt. Alexander and his companions were forced to wage siege warfare against seven cities, particularly against the mightiest of them, Cyropolis, built by Cyrus the Great.

Their inhabitants were mercilessly handled: death for the men, slavery for the women and children, and deportation to newly colonized regions.

Faced with this offensive, the Scythian populations on the far side of the Jaxartes were struck with fear. With many of them living the nomadic life, they were afraid that a new conqueror was approaching, intent on upsetting their traditional dealings with sedentary populations. Against all advice Alexander decided to cross the river. His lightning-swift punitive foray

A hoard of gold and silver objects found late in the 19th century on the banks of the Oxus gives us a priceless view of the close links between sedentary societies of northwest India and the nomadic Scythians of the steppes. This golden chariot (below) drawn by four horses is a miniature version of the battle-chariots used by the steppe nomads. The 5th-century BC historian Herodotus said the Scythians of Europe (Ukraine) lived in "portable houses on wheels."

convinced the chieftain of the Scythian tribes to sue for peace. The following year, 328 BC, his successor offered to seal his friendship with Alexander by means of a marriage. Nothing came of the proposal, but there were no further wars with the Macedonians.

Attacks against Alexander came thick and fast, and on several fronts at once

While Alexander was facing down the Scythian threat, Spitamenes laid siege to Maracanda. Alexander sent a force of 1,400 cavalry and 1,500 infantry against him, and their leaders hurled them into a reckless assault. In the ensuing disaster, his soldiers were cut to pieces in the valley of the Zarafshen River.

It was the Macedonians' first real defeat in open battle. The situation was made even more difficult by Spitamenes's consistent refusal to be drawn into a set confrontation. As this defeat was likely to have negative repercussions on army morale, Alexander concealed the disaster and, on pain of death, forbade the survivors to divulge the truth.

In Sogdiana too, resistance grew up around local princelings who controlled lands, armies raised from their peasantry, and fortified citadels.

Scythian horse-men (above) formed an elite component of the Great King's armies; they had even fought in Greece during the Median Wars. Darius III used them at the battle of Gaugamela. For a time, Scythian units fought alongside Bessus and Spitamenes before coming over to Alexander.

Only by fighting throughout the year 328 did Alexander finally overcome them—just as Spitamenes himself disappeared, eliminated by his own allies. Seeing the fate of those who resisted, however, many noblemen yielded to Alexander and in return were allowed to keep their lands and fortunes.

Henceforth a ghost would haunt the king—Cleitus, his lifelong friend

The growing number of Persian courtiers around the king angered some Macedonian nobles. During a banquet at Samarkand, where the drinking was heavy, Cleitus—the king's foster brother—took the floor to accuse Alexander of turning into a Persian-style despot and forgetting the ways of Macedonian royalty. He reminded Alexander that as king he was honor-bound to observe a certain respect in his relations with the nobility. Seized by uncontrollable rage, Alexander killed Cleitus with his own hands. Immediately after his impetuous deed, the king was full of remorse. According to some accounts, he tried to kill himself with the spear he had just used on Cleitus, but his men prevented him. Alexander—rather dramatically—mourned the loss of his general, and his friends comforted him. But all knew that Cleitus had been killed for daring to criticize the king.

Despite criticism Alexander continued his policy of collaboration with the Persians

The most glittering symbol of the Greco-Persian

Some Scythian tribes living beyond the Jaxartes were subjects of the Great King. In 516–15 BC, Darius I had conquered their king, Shunka, shown above in the line of captive rebel kings on the cliff at Bisutun. He is identifiable by his pointed headgear, which gave the Scythians the name by which the Persians knew them: "arrow-bonneted Scythians."

In 327, to cement his union with the Iranian nobility, Alexander decided to contract a highly symbolic marriage with Roxane, a Persian princess of exceptional beauty (opposite, depicted in a Renaissance painting). He persuaded several of his companions to take Bactrian princesses as wives, as well. The ceremony was sumptuous but celebrated Macedonian style, clearly indicating that the marriage did not imply any kind of fusion with the conquered Persians. Indeed, as a security measure, the Iranian nobles who had joined him were obliged to provide hostages: for example Oxyartes, Roxane's father, had to release two of his sons to accompany the conqueror to India.

"Wholly consumed by desire, Alexander ordered bread brought in, according to his native custom; this for the Macedonians was the holiest symbol of carnal union; it was cut with a sword and each spouse ate of it.... In this way, the king of Asia and of Europe was joined in marriage to a captive who would give him a child who would lord it over the victors."

Quintus Curtius
History of Alexander,
1st century AD

partnership was Alexander's marriage in the winter of 328–27 to Roxane, daughter of the Bactrian nobleman Oxyartes.

Shortly afterward, however, fresh opposition surfaced, this time in the person of Aristotle's nephew Callisthenes. It was triggered by Alexander's orders that everyone, Macedonians and Persians alike, should adopt the Persian custom of *proskynesis*, or making a gesture of obeisance, when received into audience with him. Clearly, many Macedonians were outraged—and humiliated—at this new-found formality with their king. Alexander imprisoned and then executed Callisthenes, but very wisely stopped insisting on the contentious gesture.

All possible steps were taken to maintain order in the conquered territories and to raise new forces there

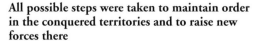

Alexander now founded several cities, intended as much for military as political ends, as well as colonies and garrisons (the latter being wholly military), and set them under the authority of a satrap with Greek and Macedonian generals. He also levied 30,000 young men in the conquered lands, ordering them to appear before him fully armed: This was a tactic to forestall any uprising in his rear, with the young recruits filling the dual role of hostages and soldiers. Finally, he left 15,000 men with the Macedonian Amyntas, now satrap of Bactria.

He needed to raise still more troops before leaving for India. He had suffered heavy losses in the course of his hard-fought campaigns; there had been many desertions, and his units had been still further weakened by the settlement of several thousand Greeks and Macedonians in his new cities and military colonies. His reinforcements (20,000 men recruited in Greece and Asia Minor in the winter of 329–28) did not make up for those losses any more than they allowed him to assemble a powerful army for the planned Indian expedition. He was therefore forced to raise troops locally.

Alexander hoped for a new generation of soldiers to man the empire

Equally concerned with building the future, Alexander urged his soldiers to marry their Asian concubines, partly to dull their longing for their homeland but also to produce a new generation of young men who could be recruited in their turn. Given these circumstances, the army that set out for India was markedly different from the one that had landed seven years earlier in Asia Minor. In addition to the Macedonians and Greeks, it now numbered Scythians and other horsemen raised in Bactria, Sogdiana, Arachosia, or the Parapamisadae. Alexander had thus achieved his twin objectives: making use of the Persians without depriving the Macedonians of their status as a conquering people.

Founded by Alexander in northern Afghanistan, Ai Khanoum preserved its character as a Greek settlement until its destruction in 145 BC. Far left: The silver plate excavated from one of its temples depicts the goddess Cybele on her chariot drawn by lions. The mountainous landscape is dominated by the Sun, the Moon, and a Star. One priest holds a parasol over the goddess, while another places an offering on an altar.

Alexander adapted the ceremonies of the Persian court for his own ends. Left: Seated majestically on his throne, the Great King receives a distinguished visitor who must blow him a kiss with his right hand while bowing from the waist. This was one of the gestures that the Greeks called *proskynesis,* or obeisance, which they saw—incorrectly— as a gesture implying royal divinity.

In 516–15 Darius I had made himself master of Gandhara, but in the ensuing two centuries Achaemenid authority had waned. In 326 several Indian kingdoms carved up for themselves the lands of the upper Indus River valley and its tributaries. It was Alexander's ambition to restore Persia's former sovereignty—to his own advantage.

CHAPTER V

FROM THE INDUS TO THE PERSIAN GULF

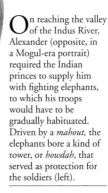

On reaching the valley of the Indus River, Alexander (opposite, in a Mogul-era portrait) required the Indian princes to supply him with fighting elephants, to which his troops would have to be gradually habituated. Driven by a *mahout,* the elephants bore a kind of tower, or *howdah,* that served as protection for the soldiers (left).

Alexander assessed the situation

Before launching into his Indian venture, Alexander made sure of the support of the rajah of Taxila (in modern Pakistan), who, with the rulers Abisares and Porus, dominated the political scene in these territories. He therefore acquainted himself with the various rivalries tearing the region apart: tension between Porus and the ruler of Taxila, and the existence of independent peoples and cities.

On its departure from Nicaea, where the Macedonians had wintered, the army was split in two. Perdiccas and Hephaestion, accompanied by the rajah of Taxila, were ordered to travel up the Kabul River to "pacify"

The Khyber Pass (above) commands the route from Pakistan to Afghanistan.

Gandhara (part of modern Afghanistan and Pakistan) and to reach the valley of the Indus along the traditional caravan road, which even today is one of the ways of reaching Pakistan from Afghanistan.

Alexander himself took the rest of the army with him in an assault on the valleys of the Lower Himalayas

Alexander's task, traditionally known as "the Alpine campaign," was to subdue the mountain tribes (Aspasians, Guraians, Assacenes) who lived in the fertile valleys on the right bank of the Kabul River: Alingar, Kunar, Swat, and Penjkura. He had to pick off

Despite the elephants, Alexander's cavalry (below), strengthened by Iranian units and even by a corps of a thousand mounted Indian archers, continued to play a leading role in the campaign.

these eagles' nests one by one. They were ferociously defended by highlanders resolved to fight to the end, "barbarians," according to the ancient Indian texts. Alexander destroyed most of the cities, killing their inhabitants and leaving behind garrisons in strategic locations.

At the end of the campaign, resistance was concentrated in the forbiddingly powerful fortress of Aornos (Pir-Sar), located in a bend of the upper Indus. Once Alexander had taken it, he handed it over to the Indian prince Sisicottos, who had fought alongside him for the last few years.

Even while fighting, Alexander was mindful of his own people's interests, and of the peace they hoped to return to one day in Greece. Indeed, according to Arrian, "the Macedonians took possession of more than 230,000 oxen, of which Alexander chose the finest specimens since they seemed to him of remarkable beauty and stature and he wished to send them back to Macedonia to work the land."

Birth of a legend: the land of the "Man Who Would Be King"

Next Alexander descended the Indus as far as the designated meeting place where Hephaestion and Perdiccas awaited him. Before crossing the river by the bridge his lieutenants had built, he completed arrangements for the conquered territories. To the Macedonian Nicanor he assigned "the lands beyond the Indus." But Macedonian control would affect only the surface, and would not endure: The Indian princelings lost none of their influence, and Nicanor— like the pockets of Greek-Macedonian garrison troops Alexander left in his wake—soon vanished from the scene. But these Greeks abandoned in the lofty mountains of the Indus valley would give birth to the legend of fair-haired, blue-eyed peoples much later immortalized by the Indian-born Englishman Rudyard Kipling in his novel *The Man Who Would Be King*.

True to his word, the new rajah of Taxila, Ambhi, welcomed Alexander at the gates of his capital, an

Rivers are major obstacles to armies on the move. In those days there were few permanent bridges; units moved across at fords at low-water level, or else used pontoon bridges (opposite) of boats strung across strategic crossing-points by army engineers.

"At a given signal, the boats are cast loose and allowed to drift with the current.... As is natural, the current carries them away, but they are held back by an oared barge until they reach their assigned position. There, reed baskets filled with unquarried stones are sunk off the prow of each boat to hold it steady against the flow. Once the first boat is thus tethered, a second in its turn is anchored against the current; when the two boats are coupled together, beams are immediately thrown athwart them, the whole cemented by small planks nailed crosswise. Thus the work goes forward...."

Arrian
Campaigns of Alexander,
2d century AD

important and wealthy city, allegedly, the biggest such city between the Indus and Hydaspes. Alexander appointed a satrap, Philippos, and installed a garrison. But he let Ambhi keep his kingdom, on condition that he supply a 5,000-man contingent and accompany Alexander on the expedition.

Alexander's aim was to march against the Indian King Porus, crossing the Hydaspes River at the height of the summer monsoon

It was a grueling, punishing campaign. In spite of the guard posts Porus had established along the right bank of the river, Alexander managed to get across with 6,000 infantry and 5,000 horsemen, many of them from eastern Iran. The most remarkable of these were the famous mounted archers raised from among the Dahae, a nomadic Central Asian people.

"Porus [below, on the elephant], gathering forty beasts around him, drove at the enemy with the whole mass of his elephants and inflicted grievous losses. Moreover, he himself was far superior to his companions in arms and in physical strength. Indeed he measured [over seven feet, or two meters] high, so that he hurled his javelins with the strength of a catapult."

Diodorus Siculus
Historical Library,
1st century BC

"Seized around the waists by the elephants' trunks and tossed into the air, some soldiers met a horrible death. Many others also met their deaths, thrust through by the animals' tusks, their bodies pierced by wounds." (Arrian)

In the pitched battle that soon followed, Porus was confident that his 300 chariots and 200 war elephants—deployed ahead of his front line—would carry the day. But the chariots quickly bogged down in the sodden soil of the battlefield and were useless against the Macedonian troops. However, many

"Losses in the Indian infantry amounted to 20,000, or very nearly, the cavalry lost around 3,000, and all the chariots were destroyed. Porus's two sons were killed. So were the commanders of the elephant and chariot regiments as well as every general in Porus's army."

Arrian
Campaigns of Alexander,
2d century AD

soldiers perished under the pachyderms' hooves despite the efforts of Alexander's spearmen and archers, who concentrated their fire on the elephants' riders, or *mahouts.*

In the thick of the fighting, Porus himself was mounted on an elephant of enormous size. Wounded several times, he at last agreed to surrender. The ancient authors point again and again to Alexander's generosity in allowing Porus to keep his crown and his kingdom. But yet again, this generosity was politically driven—for Alexander had neither the means nor the desire to occupy and hold down Porus's kingdom.

While the king of Taxila had submitted to Alexander, Porus was determined to vanquish him in battle in order to preserve his independence and gain the upper hand throughout northern India. The silver ten-drachma coin below depicts the battle as a duel between the two kings—one astride his horse, the other mounted on an elephant.

Backed by this new ally, who now reinforced him with 5,000 Indians and dozens of elephants, Alexander continued his eastward drive

Bolstered by the optimistic information Porus was giving him, Alexander quickly forded the rivers Akesines (the Chenab) and Hydraotes (the Ravi), subduing cities, peoples, and kings, and leaving garrisons behind him. Only when he reached the banks of the Hyphasis (the Beas) did he learn the unpleasant truth about the regions he planned to conquer. Beyond the river lay a twelve-day march across the Thar Desert before he reached another river, the Ganges, which was more than three miles (5½ kilometers) across. On the other side he would be confronted by the powerful king of Maghada, a member of the great Nanda dynasty, at the head of an immense army boasting 2,000 chariots and 4,000 elephants caparisoned for war. Despite this alarming news, brought to him by King Phegeus, Alexander remained determined to ford the Hyphasis.

"Alexander went out ahead of his army and rode to meet Porus with a handful of companions [opposite]. Pulling up his steed, he marveled at the king's stature, his beauty, his look of untamed determination: It was one brave man encountering another. Then Alexander asked him how he wished to be treated. And Porus answered: 'Like a king!'"

Arrian
Campaigns of Alexander,
2d century AD

Eight years of war and weariness

For or the first time, Alexander's soldiers began to question his orders.

Sensing the opposition, he called his men together. With all the eloquence and charisma at his command he tried to revive their energy and their enthusiasm for new conquests—in vain: There was not a soldier who uttered a word in response.

Pushed forward by his companions, the veteran officer Coenus gave voice to their troubled feelings. He began by recalling all those who had died in battle and above all those who had succumbed to wounds or disease. Compared to those thousands left along their trail, only a tiny handful of survivors remained. The men of 334 BC who were still by Alexander's side had covered more than 12,500 miles since Troy. Coenus explained how all of them, without exception, longed to see their families again, their wives and their children, and needless to say the soil of their native land. He spoke, too, of the soldiers left behind in the colonies, remaining there against their will. And had not the king himself ordered the execution in India of one of his companions, Menander, whom he had appointed governor of a fortress against the man's own wishes? Coenus ended his speech to the frenzied applause of the army.

The next day Alexander yielded. His decision was greeted with cries of joy; a host of weeping soldiers approached the royal tent, calling down blessings on Alexander for having agreed to agree to bring an end to his conquests for their sake.

To publicize Alexander's victories in India, his successors often had him depicted with his head covered in an elephant's hide and tusks (above).

"The young conquering king lorded it over all this captive people, vanquished and groveling at his feet…. The little Indian valley where his immense and magnificent throne was established contained all of India, the temples with their fantastic roofs, the glaring idols, the sacred lakes, the underground caves full of mysteries and terror. And Greece, the soul of radiant prideful Greece, triumphed from afar in these unexplored zones of dream and mystery."
Gustave Moreau

On the banks of the Hyphasis, twelve enormous altars were set up to mark the farthest extent of the conquests

Thus the army turned back, and Alexander

set up camp on the banks of the Hyphasis, near two cities he had founded on either shore: One dedicated to Athena Nike, goddess of Victory, the other to the memory of his horse Bucephalus, who had followed him throughout the Asia campaign and died of old age at thirty. Only Porus drew lasting benefit from the campaign. He was designated "king of all conquered India," with the obligation to pay a tribute to the Macedonian satrap Philippos, the king's representative for the whole territory between Gandhara and the Hyphasis.

Victory over Porus was the most important gain of the whole Asia campaign, coming as rumors of Alexander's death were spreading in the rear echelons. The image of the victorious young king has inspired many artists, including the 19th-century French painter Gustave Moreau (above and opposite).

Alexander decided to return by reaching the "Great Sea"—the Indus delta and the Indian Ocean—by river

He picked those of his soldiers whose origins suggested that they knew about the building and handling of ships: Phoenicians, Cypriots, Egyptians, Indians, and Hellespontines. He soon had ready a considerable fleet of around 1,000 vessels, including 80 thirty-oared ships, to transport horses and men. Meanwhile, the army had been reinforced by contingents which had come in from the west and were freshly equipped, thanks to the delivery in India of 25,000 suits of armor and weapons.

Part of the army took to the boats with Alexander; the other detachments, led by Craterus, Hephaestion, and the satrap Philippos, marched overland to the junction of the Hydaspes and the Akesines. After the customary sacrifices to the gods of seas and rivers, the flotilla moved out in November 326.

The descent of the Indus was perilous and tricky, with rapids and rough stretches posing dangers to both men and ships. Indeed, it was a military expedition rather than a cruise, for Alexander was intent on subduing all the populations he encountered on his path. Whenever he found a section of the shore where he could moor he received the submission of the Indian river-dwellers, who bound themselves to him by treaty.

Impressive though this vast convoy was, not everyone along the army's route was willing to yield without a fight

The Malli, or Malavas, living along the middle reaches of the Hydraotes, and the Oxydracae, whose territory stretched between the lower courses of the Akesines and the Hesidrus, forced Alexander to wage campaigns of extreme ferocity.

He threw several army corps in a circle around the territory of the Malavas, slaughtering every man caught unawares outside their city ramparts; the 2,000 Malavas

"The hunters drive [the captured elephants] into the villages and at first give them hay and grass to eat; but they remain downcast, refusing all food; then the Indians surround them, beating drums and cymbals and singing, and in this way they tame them. The elephant is indeed intelligent.... People tell of elephants retrieving the body of their *mahout*, slain in battle, and taking him back for burial, and of others who protect him with their body as with a wall as he lies helpless on the ground; others still have fought to protect him when he falls. One even, having slain his *mahout* in a moment of anger, soon died of despair."

Arrian
Campaigns of Alexander,
2d century AD

who held out for a while in the citadel were also put to death. Others were cut down with equal ruthlessness when they attempted to cross the Hydraotes River. One of Alexander's lieutenants reduced to slavery all the Malavas who had taken refuge in another city. Another group, which had also withdrawn into a citadel, was exterminated, while others chose suicide.

Flying columns crisscrossed the countryside to hunt down fugitives. After overcoming another city—Alexander was seriously wounded while it was under siege—his troops, according to accounts, set about killing the Indians, cutting them down without sparing either woman or child. The surviving Malavas sent ambassadors to offer surrender. Horrified, the Oxydracae followed suit.

Sind—the Lower Indus valley—still remained to be conquered

This region had been established as a satrapy entrusted to Philippos and Alexander's father-in-law Oxyartes. Before embarking on the adventure, Alexander founded another Alexandria, at the confluence of the Indus and the

When Alexander reached the Indus valley a high proportion of the local princes (*rajahs*) offered submission of their own free will, personally greeting him at the frontiers of their kingdom, or sending him ambassadors to demonstrate their desire not to resist him under arms. The king received them all in audience during his sojourn at Taxila. In the painting below we see just behind the king the man named Calanos, the most famous of Indian sages, whom the Greeks called sophists, gymnosophists, or Brahmans.

Opposite: An elephant in battle painted on a vase.

Akesines. Shortly afterward, yet another Alexandria was born on the territory of the Soghdians, grouping 1,000 settlers; a garrison was quartered in the capital of the king, Musikanos, who, on the advice of his Brahman priests, attempted an uprising. Alexander at once reacted, dispatching a punitive expedition against his kingdom, establishing further garrisons and putting Musikanos to death. New settlements went up along the left bank of the river.

Finally, in 325, Alexander made camp in Pattala, capital of the Indus delta region, which he then fortified. There he made preparations for the return journey to Persia and Babylonia. One column was entrusted to Craterus, who was ordered to lead part of the army and the elephants to Carmania along the road through Arachosia and Drangiana. Craterus therefore marched through the Bolan Pass to Kandahar, capital of Arachosia. Alexander himself, at the head of other units, was to meet him at a fixed rendezvous. The rest of the army would join them via the sea route, coming northward along the coast from Pattala into the Persian Gulf. The shipyards were kept busy refitting old vessels and building new ones.

Nearchus, already Alexander's admiral during the descent of the Indus, would be in overall command of the homebound fleet

Originally from Crete, Nearchus was a "naturalized" Macedonian. Long a companion of Alexander's, he had been appointed satrap of Lycia in 334. In his memoirs—which were used by the Roman-era historian Arrian in his influential account of the expedition—Nearchus claims, with spurious modesty, that Alexander chose him simply because he inspired confidence in his sailors and the soldiers aboard ship. And indeed he would often need to reassure soldiers alarmed at such unaccustomed phenomena as the tidal extremes of the Indus delta.

To travel south down the Indus valley, Alexander systematically used the river. He built a first fleet in 326. Not long after, the same ships were commandeered for the crossing of the Hydaspes. For that purpose, reports

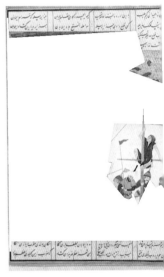

Arrian, "they were dismantled and transported, the smallest boats in two parts, but the thirty-oared vessels in three pieces, on carts as far as the banks of the Hydaspes. There the boats were reassembled and the flotilla stood ready to sail."

A few months later, in the Persian Gulf, there would be renewed panic when the flotilla encountered whales —very different creatures from the sunny-spirited dolphins of the Mediterranean.

A journey of this length presented enormous logistical problems—food supplies had to be assured, and water barrels refilled. For those marching along the coast road the journey was equally grueling

When he moved out in August 325, Alexander chose to move in step with Nearchus's fleet up the coast. In order to supply abundant water to the army, which would be sailing offshore, he ordered wells to be dug along the delta coast. He sought consistently to keep to the coastal road, watching out for harbors and making preparations for the fleet sailing alongside his path, either by assembling merchants at agreed-upon points or by preparing an anchorage. It was a challenging task, for Alexander also had to feed his own army—12,000 men—and the hundreds of women and children straggling in its wake. Gedrosia was a harsh land, and his troops were so hard-pressed by hunger and thirst that they raided the supplies intended for Nearchus's mariners! Alexander lost thousands of men. When they reached the more hospitable region of Carmania—where Craterus was waiting as planned—the survivors were able to recuperate.

Nearchus was ordered to reconnoiter the coastline, moorings, and even the smallest islands, to put in at

Later, however, Alexander decided to sail down the Hydaspes as far as "the Great Sea." He was thus following the same route as Darius I, who in 516–15 sent a river expedition to chart the mouths of the Indus before dispatching it on a dangerous circum-navigation of the Arabian peninsula to Egypt.

Left: Alexander being received by an Indian queen. Among other gifts, the Indian kings offered Alexander a young woman of wondrous beauty, a philosopher capable of answering any question, a doctor capable of curing anything except a fatal wound, and a vase which could never be drained and which instantly slaked thirst.

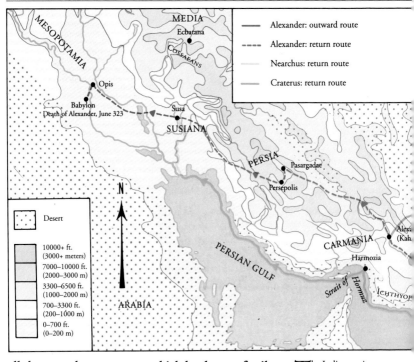

all the coastal towns, to see which lands were fertile and which desert

Nearchus waited until October, to take advantage of the monsoon winds. Avoiding the open sea, his fleet hugged the coast, weighing anchor every night in more or less well-fitted ports. The sailors were overjoyed whenever they made landfall where there was a stream or the occasional grain-depot left by Alexander. Most

The India crossing ran north-south, from the Hindu Kush to the Indian Ocean.

Below: Alexander's flotilla.

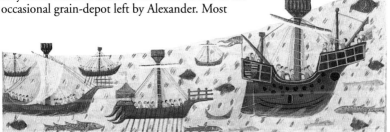

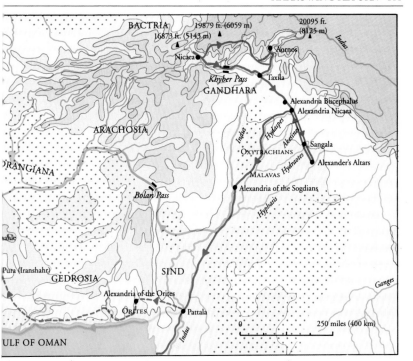

of the time, though, they had to make do with the meat of fish-fed sheep, a specialty of the desolate land of the Ichthyophagi (or fish-eaters). A raid of the local settlements yielded a meager booty consisting largely of fish-meal.

Underfed and exhausted, Nearchus's sailors also had to fight off the natives. On the coast ruled by the Orites (who had put up a stiff resistance to Alexander), they had to erect a moat and palisade around their camp.

But abundance returned when they reached Harmozeia (modern Hormuz) in Carmania, where Alexander awaited the fleet, before taking ship again, this time with a pilot, for the Euphrates. From this point on it was plain sailing. The Persian coast of the Gulf was densely populated and offered decent ports.

For the return to Persia, the army followed three routes: Craterus returned to the interior through the Bolan Pass, Quetta, and Kandahar, and marched down into Carmania. Alexander left Pattala and followed the coastline; then, having made junction with Craterus, he continued toward Persia. As for Nearchus, his fleet hugged the shoreline as far as Diridotis at the mouth of the Euphrates, then turned north to Susa—by water all the way.

After six years of absence and conquest, Alexander found his empire in serious disarray. The satraps and administrators he had left behind him had either neglected their trust or actually overstepped their powers. Alexander's first goal was therefore to restore order to the conquered cities and countries.

CHAPTER VI
FINAL YEARS, LAST DREAMS

Alexander had but two years to live in 325. He spent them traveling from one capital to another of the former Persian Empire—now his own. There remained one final journey: his own funeral procession from Babylon to Alexandria, where his tomb awaited him (although today its whereabouts remain one of the world's great archaeological mysteries).

Did the Roman emperor Augustus really visit it, as this 17th-century painting (opposite) suggests? Right: Alexander as he lay dying.

Alexander's appointees anticipated his return

Fearing the king's anger, the Macedonian Harpalus, who had been entrusted with overall administration of the treasury and finance, fled Babylonia. Along with 6,000 Greek mercenaries, he headed for Cilicia and then Greece, taking with him 5,000 talents, part of which would be used two years later by Athens to fund its rebellion against Macedonian domination.

To counter the anti-Macedonian revolutionary ferment, Alexander ordered the execution of Baryaxes, who had proclaimed himself king of the Persians and Medes. On his own homeward route, Craterus too had acted swiftly, arresting a rebellious official named Ordanes.

Among the satraps and commanders of the occupation forces, Cleander, Sitalces, and Heraklon, the generals of Media, were accused of gross misconduct by the inhabitants of Media and by their own troops: looting of temples, violation of ancient graves, violence against women of the Median nobility. Heraklon was accused of ransacking one of the temples of Susa. All three were executed. Alexander was anxious to set an example, to overawe the other satraps—as well as the local aristocracy, whose support remained as vital as ever—once and for all.

It appears, however, that the ruling classes of the conquered regions had made no concerted attempt at revolt. What they chiefly expected of the king was confirmation of a policy founded on understanding and cooperation.

Once again, Alexander called a halt at Pasargadae and Persepolis

Arrian reports that at this point the king still felt great regret at having burned down the royal palace of Persepolis in 330. In 325 he took a series of highly symbolic steps intended to win over the Persian aristocracy and people.

Finding the tomb and sarcophagus of Cyrus at Pasargadae looted by grave-robbers, he ordered the site restored to its original condition. Although tortured, the

Determined to nip in the bud all potential bids for independence among his satraps, Alexander took extreme measures against rebels. Quintus Curtius stresses the ruthless nature of the royal retribution, depicted here by the medieval miniaturist who illustrated the Latin historian's work.

"Learning of the rebellious affair [of the generals of Media], the king announced that the prosecutors had omitted one charge: that of having despaired of his own salvation. Indeed they would never have dared essay such crimes if they had believed or desired that he would return from India safe and sound. He therefore had the accused imprisoned, and put to death six hundred of the soldiers who had served as instruments of their cruelty. The same day, those responsible for the Persian uprising were also done to death."

Quintus Curtius
History of Alexander,
1st century AD

L eft le prologue dudn̄. ꝟ. ᵐᵉ   fine autre petite faulte deve
et se tre mer sanue des fais daliꝭ.   se. quart chapitre de huit

de tous ses tuchers .vne esse def

Persian Magi (members of a priestly class) assigned to guard the site would not say who had been responsible, and were finally released. More than ever Alexander was determined to present himself as the successor to the Great Kings. He even adopted the custom of giving a gold piece to pregnant Persian women.

Since the death of the Persian satrap he had appointed in 331, the country had been governed by the Persian Orxines, who had taken over the vacant mandate of the king. Immensely wealthy, Orxines claimed descent from Cyrus. Charged by the Persians themselves with pillaging the royal tombs and temples and arbitrarily executing many Persians, he was put to death.

In January 334 Alexander and Nearchus once again entered Susa: Here the king began to make great plans for the Persian Gulf.

In February 324 a mass wedding ceremony was held at Susa

Adopting the Persian custom of polygamy, the king now married two Achaemenid princesses, while several dozen of his companions were joined in matrimony to women of the highest ranks of the Persian and Median aristocracy.

Despite the destruction wrought five years earlier, Persepolis (below) remained a city of major importance for Alexander in his ambition to be the new King of Kings. While not the capital of his new empire, Persepolis continued to be the center of the important satrapy of Persia.

"So he went to the Persian palace which he had earlier put to the torch, which I have not congratulated him for. But when he returned to the spot, Alexander himself was no longer proud of what he had done."

Arrian
Campaigns of Alexander,
2d century AD

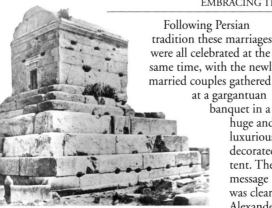

Following Persian tradition these marriages were all celebrated at the same time, with the newly married couples gathered at a gargantuan banquet in a huge and luxuriously decorated tent. The message was clear: Alexander now considered that his best means of holding on to power lay in a close alliance between the Macedonian nobility and the Persian and Median aristocracy.

By thus extending his policy of cooperation with the Persian ruling classes, Alexander alienated many of his companions and soldiers

To govern Persia in Orxines's stead Alexander appointed one of his closest companions, Peucestas, who had saved his life in the clash with the Malavas. Faithful to Alexander's own theories on how to keep

"[At Pasargadae] Alexander found Cyrus's tomb [left] emptied of everything save the sarcophagus and bed. The robbers had not even spared Cyrus's remains: they had raised the lid of the sarcophagus and thrown the body outside. They had attempted to render the sarcophagus itself easier to carry by breaking off parts of it and removing others; but having failed in this, they made their escape, leaving the sarcophagus behind them."

Arrian
Campaigns of Alexander,
2d century AD

the population submissive in all matters, the new satrap adopted the Persian language and costume, conduct which brought him great credit among the natives. Peucestas maintained this policy with such success that when in 316 he was overthrown by a successor of Alexander's, the Persian nobility reacted angrily, their spokesman declaring that they would be ruled by no other man!

Many Macedonians were shocked by Peucestas's sympathy towards the Persians, just as they had been offended by the forced marriages at Susa. They resented the fact that Iranian cavalry units had been granted the title of Companions, and that Alexander had surrounded himself with both Macedonian and Persian bodyguards.

Moreover, 30,000 young Iranians (*epigonoi*) had just arrived in Susa. Recruited by Alexander in Bactria, they had been raised in Macedonian fashion. Worse still, after watching a skillful display of their close-order maneuvers, Alexander personally rewarded the youthful recruits.

A few weeks later: crisis

When the army was drawn up at Opis on the Tigris, Alexander announced that he was sending the veterans and the wounded home. The soldiers promptly concluded that their king had decided he no longer needed them and would henceforth rely on troops recruited in the East. Alexander tried to reassure them, but his words had no effect.

As always in such cases, he retired to his tent and continued to lavish favors on the Persians. Soon contrite, the Macedonians, on their knees, begged the king to respond to their affection with his own. A sacrifice and a banquet sealed the reconciliation. Alexander prayed that he might be granted, among other benefits, harmony and good understanding between

Persian and Macedonian. And indeed it was the Macedonians who sat at the king's right hand during the ceremony.

Clearly there were limits to the policy of political cooperation with the Persians.

Reconciled with his army, Alexander was free to prepare an expedition to Arabia

His plan now was to circumnavigate the Arabian peninsula, then launch an attack on Carthage and Rome from Egypt, and finally to return to Greece from the west: Such, apparently, were the king's intentions, recorded in a document that turned up after his death. What seems certain, however, is that he was determined to subdue Arabia—in other words, the Arab coast of the Persian Gulf.

In fact, as soon as he was back in Babylonia, in early 324, he ordered boats to be built in Phoenicia and had them transported in pieces to Thapsacus on the Euphrates, and thence to a port built expressly for the purpose in Babylon. Thousands of mariners and oarsmen had been recruited in Phoenicia and along the Aegean shoreline.

According to Arrian, it was Alexander's intention "to colonize the coastal areas of the Persian Gulf, as well as the neighboring isles. He was convinced that this region could become as prosperous as Phoenicia. But his naval preparations were directed largely against the Arabs." Alexander's objectives were economic: by controlling both shores of the Persian Gulf, he would secure for himself mastery of all trade between Lower Babylonia, Arabia, and India.

Before launching on such a venture, he needed information on the topography of the country. He entrusted an initial reconnaissance probe to Archias, who was afraid to venture beyond the isle of Tylos. A second expedition, led by Androsthenes, succeeded in circumnavigating part of the peninsula. Hiero of Solis, leading the third expedition, was ordered to circumnavigate Arabia all the way to Egypt, following the course set in 512 BC by Darius's ships, which sailed from the Nile to Susa, taking the Nile

"Perhaps I have gained all this simply by issuing orders? But who among you feels that he has endured more on my behalf than I on his? Come now! Let him who has received scars display them, and I shall show mine in my turn! I have been wounded for your glory, for your prosperity! … And I was now planning to send back those no longer fit for service, making them a subject of envy to those who have remained at home; but since you all wish to go home, then go!' Having spoken thus, [Alexander] returned to his palace and removed himself from the sight of all his companions. On the third day he summoned into his presence the cream of the Persians and awarded them command of his regiments. When [the Macedonians] learned what was happening with the Persians…they hastened to the palace, [crying out] that they would remain at its doorway until Alexander took pity on them. [Seeing this], Alexander emerged, and he too began to shed tears."

Arrian
Campaigns of Alexander,
2d century AD

Opposite: Alexander as the Roman war god Mars

Canal and the Red Sea and then turning into the Persian Gulf.

Hiero shrank before the demands of the task; nevertheless, he sailed as far as the headlands which Nearchus's mariners had seen on their voyage home— the Oman peninsula at the mouth of the gulf. Sailing orders for the whole fleet were not expected until June 323.

Moving from capital to capital, from Susa to Babylon, from Babylon to Ecbatana, Alexander redoubled his tireless activity

There was no project he was not involved in: issuing instructions to his financial managers, altering the course of the Euphrates and Tigris to make them navigable for his fleet, receiving the embassies that crowded in from all sides, administering justice, monitoring official correspondence, not to speak of supervising an accelerating cycle of feasts and banquets.

In the autumn of 324 he went to Ecbatana, where Hephaestion—his dearest friend, the man on whom he had conferred the Achaemenid title of *chiliarch*— died. Although overwhelmed by grief, the king had to keep constantly on the move, his mind forever on war. First he mounted an attack on the still-unsubdued Cossaeans of Luristan. In the spring of 323 he was back in Babylon, where several Greek ambassadors awaited him.

As Alexander well knew, many of the Greek cities believed the time for revenge had come: Some of them—led by Athens—were busily recruiting Greek mercenaries who had been made masterless by the ejection of the Persian satraps who had formerly employed them. The edict which Alexander promulgated at Olympia the year before had had repercussions in Greece: "King Alexander to the exiled Greeks: We were not responsible for your banishment, but we will be responsible for your return to your several homelands."

While the royal decree had inspired the Greek exiles, it had caused disturbances in the cities. The Athenians,

For his great friend Hephaestion, the king ordered a gigantic and sumptuously decorated funeral pyre (above).

egged on by Demosthenes, now awaited their chance to rebel against the Macedonian yoke.

Following a banquet on 3 June 323, Alexander was struck down by a raging fever

After deciding that the Arab expedition would leave between 22 and 23 June, Alexander took to his bed and rested. His fever rose and fell. Nearchus, commander of the fleet, came to report on last-minute preparations. The king continued to make decisions. But his health deteriorated, and soon he lost the ability to speak. His death throes lasted several days. On the evening of 13 June, amid his soldiers' despairing cries, he died. Rumors of poison quickly spread, and some accused the Macedonian general Antipater. But the cause of

"As Alexander was departing this world at Babylon (below) his friends asked him who should inherit his kingdom. 'The strongest,' he replied. 'I foresee a great funeral contest over me.' And exactly that took place, for the most illustrious of his friends fell apart in quarrels over who should have first place, and engaged in many combats after his death."
Diodorus Siculus
Historical Library,
1st century BC

The Sidon Tomb

Nineteenth-century excavation of the royal necropolis at Sidon revealed several tombs of local kings. One of them—traditionally known as Alexander's Tomb—is embellished with several battle and hunting scenes. One carved panel depicts a Macedonian horseman in a lion's-head helmet (near left). This is believed to be Alexander, astride his mount, which rears over a Persian whose own horse has collapsed. The scene represents an idealized and often-told episode, evoking the king's valor on the battlefield. After the battle of Issus, Sidon voluntarily surrendered to Alexander, who awarded its throne to Abdalonymes. It was probably the latter who commissioned a Greek artist to design the sarcophagus and illustrate it with scenes celebrating the conqueror's feats.

War and the Hunt

Alongside the battle scenes, the artist devoted several panels of the tomb to depictions of the hunt—an activity symbolic of royal power for both Macedonians and Persi███t also provided an excellent opportunity to achieve distinction in the king's eyes. These hunts were organized in game reserves stocked with animals of every species: lion, panther, deer, and many others, which were hunted down in vast, well-planned drives. Quintus Curtius, for example, reports that in the course of one hunt in a Bactrian game reserve Alexander and his retinue killed more than 4,000 wild beasts. The scenes on the sarcophagus probably represent a royal hunt organized in some Persian "paradise" garden, or game reserve, near Sidon, when one of the king's companions, Lysimachus was seriously mauled ███ion. Worth noting ███the fact that—in marked contrast to the battle scenes— Persians and Macedonians are shown hunting their prey shoulder to shoulder. The artist thus presents a symbolic picture of the Macedonian-Iranian political collaboration that Alexander sought.

his death was probably more natural—malaria.

Quarrels over the succession at once broke out. Apart from an epileptic half-brother, Alexander left no direct heir. The inheritance would therefore be fought over by his principal Companions. Perdiccas claimed that the dying king had personally given him the ring bearing the royal seal.

First, though, the funeral ceremonies had to be held, and general mourning was declared—Persian-style—throughout the empire. Preparations began for building a funeral bier to transport the royal remains to the former Macedonian capital of Aegae. But the Macedonians would not be allowed to pay final homage to their king, for after a swift tactical move by one of his generals, Ptolemy, the conqueror was finally buried at Alexandria in Egypt.

Alexander, last of the Achaemenids

In about ten years, Alexander had not only vanquished the Great King and his armies, he had re-created the empire to his own advantage within the boundaries bequeathed to him by its Achaemenid builders. But the immensity of this achievement could not conceal its fragility.

The conqueror's death triggered a period of accelerating disintegration of the monolithic structures he had created. The royal succession was indeed conferred on Philip Arrhidaeus, Alexander's feeble-witted half-brother, and on the son born to Alexander and Roxane after the king's death.

But soon Alexander's chief generals were quarreling over territories and populations. In 306 old Antigonus the One-Eyed became the first of them to proclaim himself king; the other rivals quickly followed suit. The myth of the unity of Alexander's empire was shattered.

In the Middle East the new kings swiftly abandoned Alexander's Iranian policies. By the middle of the 3rd century BC most of the Iranian plateau was free of control by Alexander's successors in the region, the Seleucid kings. Even though the dynasty was born of a mixed Iranian-Macedonian marriage, the Seleucid

After Alexander's death, his Middle Eastern conquests were parceled out under the sway of two major dynasties: one founded by Ptolemy in Egypt, the other by Seleucus in the territories from Asia Minor to the Indus. According to custom, both kings at once minted coins struck with their own image (upper coin, above: Ptolemy; lower: Seleucus).

kingdom—like its rivals—was Greek, with its ruling class and its official language imported from Europe by the conquerors.

Greek civilization now extended as far east as Bactria and India, but this cultural expansion remained relatively superficial, failing to exert lasting influence on local peoples and their beliefs. In western Iran, and particularly in Persia, the rebirth of the Iranian Empire was already under way. Under the Sassanid dynasty, it would form the new empire of the Great King.

"First they fashioned a plate of beaten gold molded to the form of the body. Above it was placed a golden lid.... Then they were shown the bier intended to transport the remains, its top adorned with mother-of-pearl studded with precious stones. The peristyle was embellished with columns of the Ionian order.... In all, sixty-four mules were required to pull it."

Diodorus Siculus
Historical Library,
1st century BC

On transporte le Corps d'Alexandre de Babylone en Égypte (d'après la description de Diodore de Sicile)

DOCUMENTS

Alexander's historians

Although more than twenty of his contemporaries chronicled Alexander's life and campaigns, none of these texts survive in original form. Many letters and speeches attributed to Alexander are ancient forgeries or reconstructions inspired by imagination or political motives. The little solid documentation we possess from Alexander's own time is mainly to be found in stone inscriptions from the Greek cities of Europe and Asia.

B elow: Alexander the Great in an engraving.

The inscription below recalls the conditions imposed on the cities and peoples who joined the Corinthian League in 338 BC.

I swear by Zeus, Gaia, Helios, Poseidon, Athena, and Ares, by all gods and goddesses, that I will maintain peace and will not break the treaties concluded with Philip of Macedon; I will not bear arms with intent to injure, nor against those who keep their word, on land or at sea. I will not take in war any city, garrison, or port belonging to those who participate in the peace, whether by cunning or invention. I will overthrow neither the kingship of Philip and his descendants, nor the constitutions in force among the participants at the time they swore the oaths of peace. I will not act against the treaties, nor allow any other to do so, as far as I am able. If any shall do anything whatsoever contrary to these oaths and treaties, I will provide all the succor the victim asks, and I will fight any who breaks the common peace, according to the decisions of the common council and the commands of the *hegemon*.

Text of the Treaty of Corinth

An inscription from the island of Chios, in the Aegean, reproduces a letter sent to the island in 332 BC, stipulating the conditions for its return to the Macedonian sphere of influence after a brief conquest by the Persians.

Under the generalship of Deisitheus, a letter from King Alexander to the people of Chios. All those exiled from Chios shall return and Chios shall have a democratic government. Recorders shall be elected to transcribe and amend the laws so that nothing shall stand against democracy or the return of the exiles; these amendments shall be submitted to Alexander. The people of Chios shall furnish from their own purses twenty triremes [ships] with their crews, these triremes are to sail in the service of the Greek fleet. Of the ones who delivered the city to the Barbarians, those who departed shall be exiled from all cities observing the peace and arrested, in conformity with the decision of the Hellenes; all those who remained shall be led to judgment before the sanhedrin [council] of the Hellenes. If a grievance arise between the former exiles and the people of the city, it shall be referred to our judgment. Until such time as the people of Chios are reconciled, they shall have in their midst a garrison loyal to King Alexander, as numerous as is necessary, and maintained at the expense of the people of Chios.

Letter from Alexander to the people of Chios

In the Roman era, when military leaders and emperors were eager to cloak themselves in Alexander's glory, several authors wrote accounts of his conquests based on primary sources now lost to us. In the 2d century AD, Arrian, a Roman senator from the Greek-speaking East, wrote a work on Alexander. He explains the reasons for his choice of subject.

Alexander, so the story goes, blessed Achilles for having Homer to proclaim his fame to posterity. Alexander might well have counted Achilles happy on this score, since, fortunate as Alexander was in other ways, there was a great gap left here, and Alexander's exploits were never celebrated as they deserved,

either in prose or verse; there were not even choral lyrics for Alexander as for Hiero, Gelo, Thero and many others not to be compared with him, so that Alexander's exploits are far less known than very minor deeds of old times. Why, the march up into Asia of the Ten Thousand with Cyrus against King Artaxerxes, the sufferings of Clearchus and those captured with him, and the descent to the sea of those Ten Thousand under the leadership of Xenophon, are, thanks to Xenophon, far better known to the world than Alexander and Alexander's exploits. Yet Alexander did not take the field in another's army; he did not flee from the Great King, defeating only those who tried to stop the march down to the sea; no other single man performed such remarkable deeds, whether in number or magnitude, among either Greeks or barbarians. That, I declare, is why I myself have embarked on this history, not judging myself unworthy to make Alexander's deeds known to men. Whoever I may be, this I know in my favour; I need not write my name, for it is not at all unknown among men, nor my country nor my family nor any office I may have held in my own land; this I do set on paper, that country, family, and offices I find and have found from my youth in these tales. That is why I think myself not unworthy of the masters of Greek speech, since my subject Alexander was among the masters of warfare.

Arrian,
Campaigns of Alexander,
I.12.1–5,
2d century AD,
trans. P. A. Brunt

Arrian justifies his historical approach.

Wherever Ptolemy son of Lagus and Aristobulus son of Aristobulus have both given the same accounts of Alexander son of Philip, it is my practice to record what they say as completely true, but where they differ, to select the version I regard as more trustworthy and also better worth telling. In fact other writers have given a variety of accounts of Alexander, nor is there any other figure of whom there are more historians who are more contradictory of each other, but in my view Ptolemy and Aristobulus are more trustworthy in their narrative, since Aristobulus took part in king Alexander's expedition, and Ptolemy not only did the same, but as he himself was a king, mendacity would have been more dishonourable for him than for anyone else; again, both wrote when Alexander was dead and neither was under any constraint or hope of gain to make him set down anything but what actually happened. However, I have also recorded some statements made in other accounts of others, when I thought them worth mention and not entirely untrustworthy, but only as tales told of Alexander. Anyone who is surprised that with so many historians already in the field it should have occurred to me to compose this history should express his surprise only after perusing all their works and then reading mine.

Arrian,
Campaigns of Alexander,
Preface,
2d century AD,
trans. P. A. Brunt

Plutarch, the Greek contemporary of the Roman emperors Trajan and Hadrian,

A rrian depicts Alexander as a superhuman hero—basing himself partly on the memoirs of Ptolemy I, the Macedonian general who became king of Egypt. Arrian rationalized this with the assertion that a king's testimony cannot be questioned.

explains why he chose to write a history of Alexander based on his subject's character.

It being my purpose to write the lives of Alexander the king, and of Caesar, by whom Pompey was destroyed, the multitude of their great actions affords so large a field that I were to blame if I should not by way of apology forewarn my reader that I have chosen rather to epitomise the most celebrated parts of their story, than to insist at large on every particular circumstance of it. It must be borne in mind that my design is not to write histories, but lives. And the most glorious exploits do not always furnish us with the clearest discoveries of virtue or vice in men; sometimes a matter of less moment, an expression or a jest, informs us better of their characters and inclinations, than the most famous sieges, the greatest armaments, or the bloodiest battles whatsoever. Therefore as portrait-painters are more exact in the lines and features of the face, in which the character is seen, than in the other parts of the body, so I must be allowed to give my more particular attention to

P lutarch (above, in an imaginary portrait) wrote biography, rather than history.

the marks and indications of the souls of men, and while I endeavour by these to portray their lives, may be free to leave more weighty matters and great battles to be treated by others.

Plutarch,
"Life of Alexander,"
I.1–3,
1st–2d century AD,
trans. John Dryden

Diodorus, a Sicilian Greek historian of the 1st century BC and a contemporary of Julius Caesar and Augustus, outlines his goals in his introduction to Book XVII of his Historical Library, *which he devoted to Alexander's conquests.*

In this book we shall continue the systematic narrative beginning with the accession of Alexander, and include both the history of this king down to his death as well as contemporary events in the known parts of this world. This is the best method, I think, of ensuring that events will be remembered, for thus the material is arranged topically, and each story is told without interruption.

Alexander accomplished great things in a short space of time, and by his acumen and courage surpassed in the magnitude of his achievements all kings whose memory is recorded from the beginning of time. In twelve years he conquered no small part of Europe and practically all of Asia, and so acquired a fabulous reputation like that of the heroes and demi-gods of old. But there is really no need to anticipate in the introduction any of the accomplishments of this king; his deeds reported one by one will attest sufficiently the greatness of his glory. On his father's side Alexander was a descendant of Heracles and on his mother's he could claim the blood of the Aeacids, so that from his ancestors on both sides he inherited the physical and moral qualities of greatness. Pointing out as we proceed the chronology of events, we shall pass on to the happenings which concern our history.

Diodorus Siculus,
Historical Library,
XVII.1.1–5,
1st century BC,
trans. C. Bradford Welles

Immediately after his death, artists and historians in the courts and armies of his successors contributed to the creation of a mythical Alexander, embodiment of all virtues. In the Roman era, the success of a book by Plutarch testifies to the popularity

In the introduction to his book on Alexander, the historian Diodorus Siculus represents him as a peerless leader for whom he could find no precedent in the whole sweep of world history (itself the subject of Diodorus's monumental study, known as the *Historical Library*). This 17th-century gilt-metal panel shows a triumphant Alexander.

of a myth adapted to the tastes and prejudices of Roman empire builders. Alexander had become the prototype of the great conquering hero, bringing progress and civilization to barbarian and savage peoples.

The equipment that he had from Aristotle his teacher when he crossed over into Asia was more than what he had from his father Philip....

[But the philosophers were not] continuously occupied with such tremendous wars, nor with spreading civilization among foreign princes, nor in establishing Grecian cities among savage nations, nor did they go on and on, instructing lawless and ignorant tribes in the principles of law and peace.... By these criteria let Alexander also be judged! For from his words, from his deeds, and from the instruction which he imparted, it will be seen that he was indeed a philosopher....

If you examine the results of Alexander's instruction, you will see that he educated the Hyrcanians to respect the marriage bond, and taught the Arachosians to till the soil, and persuaded the Sogdians to support their parents, not to kill them, and the Persians to revere their mothers and not to take them in wedlock. O wondrous power of Philosophic Instruction, that brought the Indians to worship Greek gods, and the Scythians to bury their dead, not to devour them!... When Alexander was civilizing Asia, Homer was commonly read, and the children of the Persians, of the Susianians, and of the Gedrosians learned to chant the tragedies of Sophocles and Euripides.... Alexander established more than seventy cities among savage tribes, and sowed all Asia with Grecian magistracies, and thus overcame its uncivilized and brutish manner of living. Although few of us read Plato's *Laws*, yet hundreds of thousands have made use of Alexander's laws, and continue to use them. Those who were vanquished by Alexander are happier than those who escaped his hand; for these had no one to put an end to the wretchedness of their existence, while the victor compelled those others to lead a happy life.... Thus Alexander's new subjects would not have been civilized, had they not been vanquished; Egypt would not have its Alexandria, nor Mesopotamia its Seleuceia, nor Sogdiana its Prophthasia, nor India its Bucephalia, nor the Caucasus a Greek city hard by; for by the founding of cities in these places savagery was extinguished and the worse element, gaining familiarity with the better, changed under its influence....

For he did not overrun Asia like a robber nor was he minded to tear and rend it, as if it were booty and plunder bestowed by unexpected good fortune, after the manner in which Hannibal later descended upon Italy.... But Alexander desired to render all upon earth subject to one law of reason and one form of government and to reveal all men as one people, and to this

Throughout the Muslim world, storytellers transformed Alexander into a mythical hero, sometimes named Ishkandar, Iskandar, Skander, or Sikander, to whom were attributed rare human and martial virtues. As a historian dedicated to the truth, however, Ibn Khaldun questioned some of these legends. This Turkish manuscript illustration depicts a battle between Alexander's and Darius's armies.

purpose he made himself conform. But if the deity that sent down Alexander's soul into this world of ours had not recalled him quickly, one law would govern all mankind, and they all would look toward one rule of justice as though toward a common source of light. But as it is, that part of the world which has not looked upon Alexander has remained without sunlight.

Therefore, in the first place, the very plan and design of Alexander's expedition commends the man as a philosopher in his purpose not to win for himself luxury and extravagant living, but to win for all men concord and peace and community of interests.

Plutarch,
"On the Fortune or the
Virtue of Alexander,"
328–30,
1st–2d century AD,
trans. Frank Cole Babbitt

In the 14th century, the Andalusian Arab historian Ibn Khaldun also pondered the ways in which history is written. In the following passage he takes issue with the manner in which one of his predecessors transmitted an improbable story about the foundation by Alexander of Alexandria in Egypt.

Very often absurdities are believed and passed on, finding acceptance through the reader's faith in his informer. For example, Al-Masudi claims that sea monsters prevented Alexander [the Great] from building the city of Alexandria. The king accordingly built a wooden box containing a glass chest, entered it and descended to the bottom of the sea. There he sketched these devilish monsters. [Back again on dry land], he ordered metal copies of these monsters made, and commanded them to be lined up in front of the sites of the buildings he planned to erect in Alexandria. When the monsters rose to the surface and saw their own images they turned tail and fled, allowing the building to go forward.

This is truly the tale of a dreamer! And for several reasons. First, who would believe that Alexander could have taken a glass chest and personally braved the sea and its waves? Kings do not take such risks. If one of them ever launched upon such a foolhardy venture he would encompass his own ruin, for his subjects would rebel and overthrow him. They would not even await his return.

Furthermore, genies are not known by specific features and forms, since they are able to assume whatever shape they will. We must not take literally what is written about their many heads: for this is simply a way of inspiring horror and fear.

We thus see how questionable is Al-Masudi's tale. But that is not all. There is a material phenomenon which demonstrates the physical impossibility of the whole story. Whosoever dived beneath the sea, even inside a chest, would feel the air needed for his natural respiration grow thin. His "[vital] spirit" would swiftly become overheated. For want of the cool air necessary for a balance between the humor of the lungs and the heart's pulse he would at once perish. It is thus that people die in a bath house that is not ventilated. Those who descend to the bottom of wells or of cellars suffocate when the air is heated by miasmas and there is no way of ventilating it: they die at once. For the same reasons the fish dies when removed from the water, for the outside air does not suffice to maintain the equilibrium of his lungs. The fish is extremely warm, and the water balancing his humor is cold. Since the atmosphere of the outer air is warm it overwhelms the animal spirits and the fish quickly expires. The same holds true for sudden deaths.

Ibn Khaldun,
Treatise on Universal History,
c. 1375

During the conquest of eastern Iran and Afghanistan, Alexander settled many Greek and Macedonian soldiers in cities built on Greek plans. From these arose Greco-Bactrian kingdoms. The art of Gandhara bears witness to the close cultural contacts between Greece and India. Above: a Seated Buddha with features and clothing reflecting both Greek and Indian sculptural styles.

Alexander's successors

Alexander's sudden death in Babylon triggered a complex succession struggle. In the absence of an unquestioned heir, the conflicting ambitions of the dead king's chief lieutenants rose to the surface.

A stone medallion of Alexander.

A preliminary decision confirms Perdiccas's authority.

Alexander's generals were worthy to aspire to his throne, for they possessed such courage and inspired such respect that it would be easy to take them all for kings. Such was the beauty of their forms, the greatness of their stature and the extent of their strength and wisdom that if one did not know them one might believe that they had been chosen, not from a single nation but from all the universe. Never before had Macedonia or any other country seen the blossoming of so many illustrious men. First Philip, and then Alexander, had selected them with such care that they seemed to have sought out not companions in war so much as successors to their power. Who then could wonder that with such servants Alexander conquered the world, given that the Macedonian army was led not by so many chiefs but by so many kings? They would have been without peers if they had not fallen to fighting among themselves, and the province of Macedonia would have had many Alexanders had fortune—inspiring rivalry in courage among them—not armed them for their mutual ruin.

Moreover, if Alexander's death caused them joy it also troubled their sleep; for all of them aspired to the same rank, and...none among them so far surpassed the others that they would agree to defer to him. They therefore assembled, fully armed, in the palace to attempt to settle among themselves the manner in which the State would be governed. Perdiccas proposed that they await the confinement of Roxane, the wife of Alexander, which was imminent, for she had passed her eighth month of pregnancy; and if she gave birth to a son, to accept him as his father's successor. Meleager however argued that…they should not await the birth of a king when those already born could be chosen. If they wanted a child, there was a son of Alexander at Pergamum borne him by Barsine and bearing the name of Hercules; if they preferred a young man, there was a brother of Alexander in the camp, [Philip] Arrhidaeus, a likable prince who was acceptable to all not merely for his own name but above all for the name of his father Philip. Furthermore, Roxane was of Persian origin and it was not permissible to impose kings of the blood of those whose kingdoms they had destroyed upon the Macedonians. He added that Alexander himself had not wished it so, since he had made no mention of this child on his deathbed. Ptolemy declared himself opposed to the choice of Arrhidaeus not only because of his mother's notoriety—for she was a courtesan of Larissa—but even more because of the epilepsy afflicting him. It seemed likely that he would retain only the name of king and would abandon power to some other. It would be better to choose from among those whose merit had brought

Alexander named no heir at his death in 323 BC. Despite the charm of this 19th-century gouache, *The Wedding of Alexander,* by Johan Erdmann Hümmel, his marriage to the Sogdian princess Roxane was probably more political than romantic. But at his death she was pregnant. She gave birth to a son who reigned briefly, sharing the throne with Alexander's Macedonian half-brother Philip Arrhidaeus.

them closest to the king, who governed provinces and to whom the conduct of war was entrusted, rather than submit to unworthy men commanding in the king's name. Perdiccas's reasoning met with the approval of them all. They therefore decided to await Roxane's confinement and, should she give birth to a son, to appoint Leonnatus, Perdiccas, Craterus, and Antipater as his guardians; these were promptly accorded the oath of loyalty.

Marcus Junianus Justinus,
Epitome of the Philippic History,
XIII.1.10–15; 2.1–14,
3d century AD

The infantry, determined to preserve Macedonia's leading role in the empire, rejected this decision and promptly rebelled. The ensuing civil war—the first of many—ended with recognition of the rights of Philip Arrhidaeus, Alexander's half-brother.

The infantry—angered at being excluded from the deliberations— proclaimed Arrhidaeus, Alexander's brother, king, giving him a bodyguard chosen from their ranks and insisting that he adopt the name of Philip, his father. Hearing this, the cavalry assigned two of its leading officers, Attalus and Meleager, to calm their spirits. Flattering the throng in order to enhance their credit, they abandoned their mission and passed into the soldiers' camp. As soon as it had leadership the sedition spread. Seizing their weapons, the soldiers hastened to the palace to slaughter the cavalry. But learning of their plans, the latter hastily left the city and set up an armed camp from which they in their turn threatened the infantry. But even

among the leaders the fires of hatred could not be extinguished. Attalus despatched men to kill Perdiccas, leader of the opposition party; but since Perdiccas was armed and defied the killers, they were afraid to approach him. Such indeed was his fearlessness that he went personally to meet the infantry, and having assembled them showed them what crime they were planning: "Look," he said to them, "at the kind of men against whom you have taken up arms: They are not Persians but Macedonians; they are not enemies but your fellow citizens; many among you are even linked to them with ties of blood; and in any case they are your companions in arms, they have shared your camps and your perils. You are going to present your enemies with a fine spectacle and give them the joy of seeing all those who defeated and humiliated them fall to slaughtering one another, and you are going to sacrifice your blood to the shades of the enemies you have killed."

Perdiccas uttered these words with the rare eloquence that was one of his talents. He so moved the infantry that they accepted his advice and unanimously elected him their leader. Then the cavalry, meeting them in assembly in order to reach agreement with them, concurred with the choice of Arrhidaeus while setting aside a part of the kingdom for the son of Roxane —if she should bear a son. They deliberated before the corpse of Alexander, laid out in the midst of the assembly, so that his majesty should bear witness to their decisions.

Marcus Junianus Justinus,
Epitome of the Philippic History,
XIII.3.1–10; 4.1–4,
3d century AD

The greatest of Alexander's new cities, Alexandria in Egypt (represented allegorically here) began to play an important part in the Mediterranean region soon after its foundation. Upon Alexander's death, his general Ptolemy took military command of Egypt, which he turned into an independent kingdom.

Alexander's final plans, found in his archives after his death, revealed his ambitions.

When Perdiccas found in the memoranda of the king orders for the… designs of Alexander, which were many and great and called for an unprecedented outlay, he decided that it was inexpedient to carry them out. But that he might not appear to be arbitrarily detracting anything from the glory of Alexander, he laid these matters before the common assembly of the Macedonians for consideration.

The following were the largest and most remarkable items of the memoranda. It was proposed to build a thousand warships, larger than triremes, in Phoenicia, Syria, Cilicia, and Cyprus for the campaign against the Carthaginians and the others who live along the coast of Libya and Iberia and the adjoining coastal region as far as Sicily; to make a road along the coast of Libya as far as the Pillars of Heracles and, as needed by so great an expedition, to construct ports and shipyards at suitable places; to erect six most costly temples, each at an expense of fifteen hundred talents; and, finally, to establish cities and to transplant populations from Asia to Europe and in the opposite direction from Europe to Asia, in order to bring the largest continents to common unity and to friendly kinship by means of intermarriages and family ties. The temples mentioned above were to be built at Delos, Delphi, and Dodona, and in Macedonia a temple to Zeus at Dium, to Artemis Tauropolus at Amphipolis, and to Athena at Cyrnus. Likewise at Ilium in honour of this goddess there was to be built a temple that could never be surpassed by any other. A tomb for his father Philip was to be constructed to match the greatest of the pyramids of Egypt, buildings which some persons count among the seven greatest works of man. When these memoranda had been read, the Macedonians, although they applauded the name of Alexander, nevertheless saw that the projects were extravagant and impracticable and decided to carry out none of those that have been mentioned.

Diodorus Siculus,
Historical Library,
XVIII.4. 2–6,
1st century BC,
trans. Russel M. Geer

Alexander's successors faced multiple dangers. In Europe, the leading Greek cities, looking to Athens for leadership, attempted to free themselves from Macedonian domination. But the most pressing threat to the empire's cohesion came from the festering disagreements among its leaders. The struggle between Perdiccas and Ptolemy over Alexander's remains is a vivid illustration of this. The king's body was embalmed in Babylon.

It was the seventh day since the king's body had been lying in its coffin, for the attention of all was diverted from so solemn a duty [as the late king's funeral] to the establishment of public order. And no more burning heat exists than that of the region of Mesopotamia, so great that it destroys many animals which it overtakes on the bare ground; such is the heat of sun and sky, by which everything is burned as by fire.… I report what is recorded rather than believed: when at last his friends had leisure to care for Alexander's lifeless body, those who had entered the room saw it corrupted by no decay, nor even by the slightest discoloration. The vigour too which comes from the breath of life had not yet left his face. And so the Egyptians and Chaldeans who were ordered to care for the body after their manner, at first, as if he were still breathing, did not dare to lay their hands upon him; then after praying that it might be right and lawful for mortals to handle a god, they emptied the body of entrails, the golden coffin was filled with perfumes, and the emblem of his rank was placed upon the king's head.

> Quintus Curtius,
> *History of Alexander*,
> X.10.9–13, 1st century AD,
> trans. John C. Rolfe

A lieutenant of Perdiccas named Arrhidaeus was ordered to escort the sumptuous funeral bier to Macedonia. Ptolemy managed to circumvent him and have the conqueror buried in Egypt, where he was ruler. Diodorus Siculus gives this account.

[The funeral carriage was drawn by] sixty-four mules, selected for their strength and size. Each of them was crowned with a gilded crown, each had a golden bell hanging by either cheek, and about their necks were collars set with precious stones.

In this way the carriage was constructed and ornamented, and it appeared more magnificent when seen than when described. Because of its widespread fame it drew together many spectators; for from every city into which it came the whole people went forth to meet it and again escorted it on its way out, not becoming sated with the pleasure of beholding it. To correspond to this magnificence, it was accompanied by a crowd of roadmenders and mechanics, and also by soldiers sent to escort it.

When Arrhidaeus had spent nearly two years in making ready this work, he brought the body of the king from Babylon to Egypt. Ptolemy, moreover, doing honour to Alexander, went to meet it with an army as far as Syria, and, receiving the body, deemed it worthy of the greatest consideration. He decided for the present not to send it to Ammon, but to entomb it in the city that had been founded by Alexander himself, which lacked little of being the most renowned of the cities of the inhabited earth. There he prepared a precinct worthy of the glory of Alexander in size and construction.

Entombing him in this and honouring him with sacrifices such as are paid to demigods and with magnificent games, he won fair requital not only from men but also from the gods.

> Diodorus Siculus,
> *Historical Library*,
> XVIII.28.2–6, 1st century BC,
> trans. Russel M. Geer

The Greek historian Aelian, who lived in Rome, tells a different version of the tale.

Alexander, son of Philip and Olympias, having died at Babylon, the body of this prince who called himself a son of Jupiter lay untended while his generals quarreled over possession of his states: He was not even accorded the honors of burial offered to the basest of mortals, honors we are nature-bound to perform

A funeral chariot in the Hellenistic style. Alexander's mummified body was to be transported in such a bier, built in Babylon.

A few days after his death Alexander was embalmed by Babylonian and Egyptian experts. Perdiccas, the leader who had taken command of the empire, planned to have him buried in the royal Macedonian gravesite at Aegae. Here, in a medieval illustration to a volume of Quintus Curtius, the embalmers are at work upon the body of the king.

for the dead. Thirty days had gone by with no thought given to Alexander's funeral, before Aristander of Telmissus, moved perhaps by divine inspiration, perhaps by some other motive, stepped among the Macedonians. The gods, he told them, had revealed to him that since Alexander both in life and after death had been the most fortunate king who had ever lived, the earth which received the body where his soul had dwelt would be utterly blessed and need never fear devastation. This speech gave rise to new debate, each of them wishing to carry off to his kingdom and possess a treasure which was the guarantee of solid lasting power. Ptolemy, if certain historians are to be believed, then secretly took possession of Alexander's corpse and hastened to Egypt with it, to the city which this prince had adorned with his name. The Macedonians were unperturbed by this theft; but Perdiccas at once set off in pursuit of the robber, less exercised by his attachment to Alexander's memory or by devout respect for his remains than moved by Aristander's preaching. When Perdiccas overtook Ptolemy, they waged a battle over the corpse, a bloody battle in many ways like that at Troy…. Ptolemy, after repulsing Perdiccas, himself ordered a double of Alexander made, dressing it in royal vestments and surrounding it with the most priceless funerary ornaments; then he set it upon a Persian carriage, in a magnificent coffin embellished with gold, silver, and ivory. At the same time he sent the real body, without pomp or fanfare, along hidden and little-frequented ways. When Perdiccas had wrested Alexander's double and the carriage it rode in from Ptolemy, he believed that the prize they had fought for was his. He abandoned the chase, and did not perceive that he had been tricked until Ptolemy was beyond pursuit.

Aelian,
Various History,
XII.64, 1st–2d century AD

The precautions taken by Eumenes, who had been Alexander's record-keeper, reflect the general scramble of the generals to appropriate the dead king's crown and consolidate power.

Eumenes, who at this time also kept these things in mind, prudently made his own position secure, for he foresaw that Fortune would change again. He perceived that he himself was a foreigner and had no claim to the royal power, that the Macedonians who were now subject to him had previously decreed his death, and that those who occupied the military commands were filled with arrogance and were aiming at great affairs. He therefore understood that he would soon be despised and at the same time envied, and that his life would eventually be in danger…. Reasoning about these matters with himself, when the five hundred talents for refitting and organization were offered him in accordance with the king's letters, he at first refused to accept them, saying that he had no… desire to attain any position of command. Even now, he said, it was not of his own will that he had yielded with respect to his present office, but he had been compelled by the kings to undertake this great task…. He declared, however, that in his sleep he had seen a strange vision, which he considered it necessary to disclose to all, for he thought it would contribute much to harmony and the general good. He said that in his sleep he had seemed to see Alexander the king, alive and clad in his kingly garb, presiding over a council, giving orders to the commanders, and actively administering all the affairs of the monarchy. "Therefore," he said, "I think that we must make ready a golden throne from the royal treasure, and that after the diadem, the sceptre, the crown, and the rest of the insignia have been placed on it, all the commanders must at daybreak offer incense to Alexander before it, hold the meetings of the council in its presence, and receive their orders in the name of the king just as if he were alive and at the head of his own kingdom."

As all agreed to his proposal, everything needed was quickly made ready, for the royal treasure was rich in gold. Straightway then, when a magnificent tent had been set up, the throne was erected, upon which were placed the diadem, the sceptre, and the armour that Alexander had been wont to use. Then when an altar with a fire upon it had been put in place, all the commanders would make sacrifice from a golden casket, presenting frankincense and the most costly of the other kinds of incense and making obeisance to Alexander as to a god. After this those who exercised command would sit in the many chairs that had been placed about and take counsel together, deliberating upon the matters that from time to time required their attention. Eumenes, by placing himself on an equality with the other commanders in all the matters that were discussed and by seeking their favour through the most friendly intercourse, wore down the envy with which he had been regarded and secured for himself a great deal of good-will among the

commanders. As their reverence for the king grew stronger, they were all filled with happy expectations, just as if some god were leading them.

Diodorus Siculus,
Historical Library,
XVIII.60–61, 1st century BC,
trans. Russel M. Geer

The horrors of internecine war did not spare the members of the royal family. The two kings acknowledged at Babylon, Philip Arrhidaeus and the young Alexander IV, were at greatest risk. The former was assassinated in 317 by Alexander's mother, Olympias, who was herself murdered the following year on orders from Cassander, regent of Macedonia.

As Olympias, however, refused to flee but on the contrary was ready to be judged before all the Macedonians, Cassander, fearing that the crowd might change its mind if it heard the queen defend herself and was reminded of all the benefits conferred on the entire nation by Alexander and Philip, sent to her two hundred soldiers who were best fitted for such a task, ordering them to slay her as soon as possible. They, accordingly, broke into the royal house, but when they beheld Olympias, overawed by her exalted rank, they withdrew with their task unfulfilled. But the relatives of her victims, wishing to curry favour with Cassander as well as to avenge their dead, murdered the queen, who uttered no ignoble or womanish plea.

Such was the end of Olympias, who had attained to the highest dignity of the women of her day, having been daughter of Neoptolemus, king of the Epirotes, sister of the Alexander who made a campaign into Italy, and also wife of Philip, who was the mightiest of all who down to this time had ruled in Europe, and mother of Alexander, whose deeds were the greatest and most glorious.

> Diodorus Siculus,
> *Historical Library*,
> XIX.51.4–6, 1st century BC,
> trans. Russel M. Geer

A few years later, in 311 BC, Cassander turned his attention to the son of Alexander and Roxane.

Now Cassander perceived that Alexander, the son of Roxane, was growing up and that word was being spread throughout Macedonia by certain men that it was fitting to release the boy from custody and give him his father's kingdom; and, fearing for himself, he instructed Glaucias, who was in command of the guard over the child, to murder Roxane and the king and conceal their bodies, but to disclose to no one else what had been done. When Glaucias had carried out the instructions, Cassander, Lysimachus, and Ptolemy, and Antigonus as well, were relieved of their anticipated danger from the king; for henceforth, there being no longer anyone to inherit the realm, each of those who had rule over nations or cities entertained hopes of royal power and held the territory that had been placed under his authority as if it were a kingdom won by the spear.

> Diodorus Siculus,
> *Historical Library*,
> XIX.105.2–4, 1st century BC,
> trans. Russel M. Geer

Alexander's mother, Olympias, sought to influence politics throughout her life. The medieval picture above recalls her quarrel, exile, and reconciliation with her husband, Philip, thanks to Alexander's intercession. Exiled again after her son's death, this time to Epirus, she later returned to Macedonia to supervise the education of her grandson, and was assassinated.

Fewer than twenty years after the death of Alexander, in 306 BC, one of his marshals, Antigonus the One-Eyed, took the title of king, an example at once followed by his chief rivals. This "year of the kings" marked the end of the fiction of imperial unity.

Antigonus…was in suspense enough about the issue [of a battle of his faction against Ptolemy's forces at Cyprus], and suffered all the anxieties natural to men engaged in so perilous a struggle. And when he heard that [the envoy] Aristodemus was coming alone, it put him into yet greater trouble; he could scarcely forbear from going out to meet him himself; he sent messenger on messenger, and friend after friend, to inquire what news. But Aristodemus, walking gravely and with a settled countenance, without making any answer, still proceeded quietly onward; until Antigonus, quite alarmed and no longer able to refrain, got up and met him at the gate, whither he came with a crowd of anxious followers now collected and running after him. As soon as he saw Antigonus within hearing stretching out his hands, he accosted him with the loud exclamation, "Hail, King Antigonus! we have defeated Ptolemy by sea, and have taken Cyprus and sixteen thousand eight hundred prisoners." "Welcome, Aristodemus," replied Antigonus, "but, as you chose to torture us so long for your good news, you may wait awhile for the reward of it."

Upon this the people around gave Antigonus and Demetrius, for the first time, the title of kings. His friends at once set a diadem on the head of Antigonus; and he sent one presently to his son, with a letter addressed to him as King Demetrius. And when this news

A bronze image of Alexander from the Roman era. Alexander's proverbial beauty remained a part of his legend after his death.

From 321 to 301 BC Antigonus the One-Eyed, one of Philip II's first companions, strove to rebuild Alexander's empire. He may be the mounted Macedonian warrior depicted above, in one of the battle scenes on the famous Sidon sarcophagus. He was the first of the Macedonian generals to assume the title of king, in 306. In 301, he was eliminated by the united forces of his rivals.

was told in Egypt, that they might not seem to be dejected with the late defeat, Ptolemy's followers also took occasion to bestow the style of king upon him; and the rest of the successors of Alexander were quick to follow the example. Lysimachus began to wear the diadem, and Seleucus, who had before received the name in all addresses from the barbarians, now also took it upon him in all business with the Greeks, Cassander still retained his usual superscription in his letters, but others, both in writing and speaking, gave him the royal title. Nor was this the mere accession of a name, or introduction of a new fashion. The men's own sentiments about themselves were disturbed, and their feelings elevated; a spirit of pomp and arrogance passed into their habits of life and conversation, as a tragic actor on the stage modifies, with a change of dress, his steps, his voice, his motions in sitting down, his manner in addressing another. The punishments they inflicted were more violent after they had thus laid aside that modest style under which they formerly dissembled their power, and the influence of which had often made them gentler and less exacting to their subjects. A single flattering voice effected a revolution in the world.

Plutarch,
"Life of Demetrius,"
17–18, 1st–2d century AD,
trans. John Dryden

Alexander's legend endures

Centuries after Alexander's death, the legends of his exploits continued to be told and retold, adapted to the traditions of the many cultures he had encountered. In Arabic, Persian, and Hebrew tales (including the Old Testament) he becomes a prophet, a religious visionary, or an agent of the Devil.

Alexander was a student of one of the greatest philosophers of the classical or indeed any age, but he clearly had no taste for the contemplative life. It is interesting to try to discover in the life of this man of restless energy and unceasing action some trace of the influence of Aristotle, but it is much more likely that the young king took the mythic hero Achilles for his model. The Iliad, *especially the story of Achilles, was, we are told, one of Alexander's favorite books.*

For three years Aristotle taught Alexander and a few chosen companions at Mieza, a quiet spot remote from the distractions of the court and, we may suspect, from the influence of Olympias. About this important period of Alexander's life we are reduced for the most part to conjecture. A letter reproduced by Plutarch, in which Alexander complains to Aristotle that the publication of the *Metaphysics* has made available to all and sundry the substance of his teaching, is almost certainly a forgery. However, another letter criticizing Aristotle's teaching, which purports to have been written by the aged Isocrates, may be genuine. If it is, Aristotle will have instructed the prince in the philosophy which was taught in the Academy. Certainly, if we may judge by the number of philosophers who accompanied the expedition and by Alexander's offer of fifty talents to Xenocrates, the Academic philosopher who wrote for him a work on the duties of a king, Alexander retained an interest in the subject. Aristotle wrote a treatise *On Kingship,* perhaps for Alexander's accession, and must surely have talked to his pupil about political philosophy, but there is no indication that Alexander was in the

The lessons Alexander received at the hands of Aristotle were long thought to have made of the young prince an inquiring scientist, eager to catalogue the animal and vegetable life of the conquered territories. But Alexander did not always follow the advice of the philosopher, who had counseled him to treat his conquered enemies not as human beings but as animals or plants.

least influenced by his views on politics. Quite the reverse, in fact; for, although Aristotle had advised him to treat "barbarians" like slaves and animals, Alexander did no such thing. Doubtless, when he met these "barbarians" in the field and talked with Persian prisoners, he formed a very different opinion of their capabilities. Indeed, he may well have discounted Aristotle's teaching on this point much earlier after meeting Persian envoys and refugees who had fled to Philip's court.

But if Aristotle's teaching had little effect on his pupil's political thinking… their relationship appears to have remained cordial until the arrest and execution of Callisthenes caused a certain coolness between them.

Aristotle consolidated and extended Alexander's appreciation of Greek literature. When, after the battle of Issus, the king captured a valuable casket among Darius' baggage, he chose to keep in it a copy of the *Iliad* which Aristotle is said to have annotated for him. He is often reported to have quoted Euripides, naturally a popular author in Macedonia, and his treasurer Harpalus, when asked by Alexander to obtain books from Greece, chose the works of the three great Attic tragedians, two volumes of fourth-century poetry, and Philistus' *History of Sicily.* Earlier, Alexander had shown his reverence for Pindar by sparing the poet's house and his descendants in the sack of Thebes.

Aristotle appears to have passed on

his interest in medicine to his pupil, for Alexander did not hesitate to advise his doctors during his expedition. Again, the many scientists whom he took with him to Asia sent back to Athens much valuable data on plants and animals which enabled Theophrastus and others in the Lyceum to make great advances in botany and zoology.

J. R. Hamilton,
Alexander the Great, 1973

The text known as the Greek Alexander Romance *probably dates to the century after Alexander's death, but underwent repeated revisions for over a thousand years thereafter. In it, his deeds were transformed into the magical adventures of a fairy-tale hero.*

Some of the wise men of the kingdom came to Alexander and said, "Your majesty, we have something to show you which deserves your special attention. We will take you to the trees that speak with a human voice." So they brought Alexander to a place where there was a sanctuary of the Sun and the Moon. There was a guardpost here, and two trees closely resembling cypresses. Around these stood trees that resembled what in Egypt is called the myrrh-nut, and their fruits were also similar. The two trees in the middle of the garden spoke, the one with a man's voice, the other with a woman's. The name of the male one was Sun, and of the female one Moon....

Alexander wanted to learn more about these trees. They told him, "In the morning, when the sun rises, a voice issues from the tree of the sun, and again when the sun is in the middle of the sky, and a third time when it is about to set. And the same applies to the tree of the moon." The priests, as they evidently were, of the place came up and told Alexander, "Enter if you are

Taken captive after the Persian defeat at Issus, Sisygambis the Queen Mother remained in Alexander's retinue. Since the very earliest times, Macedonian and Greek propaganda emphasized the mother-son relationship that grew up between Alexander and the defeated queen. Her death at Susa, amid scenes of regal pomp and circumstance, was a favorite theme for artists.

pure, make obeisance and receive an oracle. And, Alexander," they went on, "no iron may be brought into the sanctuary." So Alexander ordered his men to leave their swords outside the perimeter wall. A number of men went in with Alexander, and he ordered them to explore the enclosure in all directions. He kept some of his Indian companions with him as interpreters, swearing solemnly to them that if the sun set and no oracle was heard, he would have them burnt alive.

Just then the sun set; at once an Indian voice was heard in the tree. The Indians who were with him were afraid and did not want to translate its words. Alexander became anxious and took them aside one by one. They whispered in his ear, "King Alexander, soon you must die by the hand of one of your companions." All those who stood around were extremely disturbed, but Alexander wanted to question the oracle again. As he had heard what was going to happen to him, he went in and requested that he might once more embrace his mother, Olympias. When the moon rose, its tree spoke in Greek: "King Alexander, you are to die in Babylon, by the hand of one of your companions, and you will not be able to return to your mother, Olympias."

Alexander was amazed, and wanted to bedeck the trees with the finest garlands, but the priests stopped him, saying, "This may not be. If you insist, do as you will; a king can make every law unwritten." Then Alexander was very melancholy.

At dawn he rose with the priests, his friends and the Indians, and went back to the sanctuary. After praying, he approached with one of the priests and laid his hand on the tree of the sun, and asked it if the full span of his life would be completed. That is what he really wanted to know. As the sun rose and the first rays fell on the top of the tree, a resonant voice came forth: "The span of your life is completed now, you will not be able to return to your mother, Olympias, but must die in Babylon. A short time afterwards, your mother and your wife will be horribly murdered by your own people. Ask no more about these matters, for you will be told no more."

Alexander was very unhappy when he heard this. He went out and departed from India at once, making for Persia.

The Greek Alexander Romance,
III.17, 2d century BC(?),
trans. Richard Stoneman

In the literature of medieval Europe this reinvented Alexander became a popular allegorical figure, the perfect knight—a sort of Galahad, in the chivalric manner. But for religious and moral philosophers of the Middle Ages he was more: As conqueror of the empires of the Middle East he was prophetic of Jesus's later spiritual conquest of the old dispensation. As bringer of Hellenistic Greek learning to the lands of Jewish tradition, he paved the way for Christianity. But as a ruthless assailant of the established order, his story was also sometimes interpreted in a negative light. Here, a modern scholar analyzes the complex medieval religious symbolism of Alexander.

It is, therefore, from the broken survivals of antique tradition that the conception of Alexander in the writings of medieval moralists is principally derived.… [But] The substitution of Christian for pagan ideas necessarily involved the replacement of Fortune, that controlling force in the development of Alexander's character, by Divine Providence. But in the parallel Jewish tradition, in the testimony of the Bible and of Josephus, Alexander is God's instrument of wrath against the Persians, and his career is watched over by God....

The key to this approach to Alexander lies in the view of him as a figure in world history, as the originator of an epoch and the creator of an empire which was eventually to give Antiochus his dominion over the Jews. Such a view involved, not the consideration of isolated philosophic encounters of Alexander, but the portrait of the all-conquering tyrant whose career was foreseen by Daniel, and summarized in Maccabees. Therefore the theologians went back to the historical texts for the amplification of their portrait of the historical Alexander; and especially to Orosius, who had himself presented such a portrait of Alexander in the succession of world history, and whose work was an invaluable and almost inevitable source for all later chronicle writers. Thus those theological accounts of Alexander which we have now to describe were founded upon Orosius' condemnation of Alexander in the supposed light of Scriptural allegorical interpretation....

For [Orosius] Alexander was a ruthless, blood-thirsty conqueror fired by his insane love of glory in battle. At much the same period we find the same view in Fulgentius, who combined Orosius with Julius Valerius in a vituperative attack on Alexander which was the first to be based on a combination of history and legend.... These two authors considered Alexander as the ruthless destroyer of Persia....

The two important references to Alexander in the Bible occur in Daniel and Maccabees. The first was interpreted as a prophecy of his coming and of his destruction of the Persian Empire; the other gives a brief narrative of his career of conquest as a prelude to the deeds of his disreputable successor Antiochus. These two passages were connected in the minds of Scriptural commentators and in the minds of their [medieval] readers by the similarity in both texts of the aspect of Alexander's career considered. In both it is his conquests that interest the writer.... The commentaries upon these passages, however, cannot be studied together, since the references to Alexander in Daniel are couched in prophetic and mystical language, and therefore demanded from the first a factual interpretation; while the narrative in Maccabees is historical fact, and was therefore interpreted allegorically by the twelfth-century mystics.

Alexander appears in two allegories in the book of Daniel, in the first as the third of the Four Beasts, a leopard with four wings and four heads, and in the second as a he-goat who attacks the ram with two horns and overcomes him, breaking his horns. The first writer of importance upon these passages was St. Jerome, who offered an interpretation which was almost invariably upheld by later commentators, since it is a simple matter of the interpretation of prophecy, and not, as in Maccabees, a question of finding an apposite symbolism.

When Alexander appears as the leopard, his four wings are interpreted as symbolic of the swiftness of his career of conquest, while the four heads are his four successors; as the goat, he attacks Darius, the Ram, whose two horns represent his two empires of Media and Persia, and destroys his might. These two prophetic passages, in conjunction with a later reference to the king of Greece who shall come to destroy Persia, are of very great importance in the theological conception of Alexander, for they might only be interpreted as St. Jerome interpreted them: Alexander's conquests were due not to his own power but to the will of God....

The medieval commentaries upon the opening verses of the first book of Maccabees...are of great interest, not only for the light that they throw upon the theological attitude to Alexander, but for the study in medieval symbolism that they provide. I Maccabees opens with a very brief description of Alexander's military career, telling how

Above: *Alexander's Celestial Journey,* an illustration from an Alexander romance published in Paris in 1506. Alexander, dressed as a king, is carried up into the sky high above the earth in a cage drawn by four griffins. The precise meaning of the scene is not known.

all nations stood in fear of him, how his Empire was divided after his death, and how the Jews eventually passed under the jurisdiction of the Seleucid Antiochus, the enemy and persecutor of the Maccabees and their followers. In this narrative Alexander is mentioned merely because he is the most important historical predecessor of Antiochus.

Antiochus, as the persecutor of the Jews, became from the early days of Scriptural allegory separated from his chronological setting, and appeared as the conventional type of Antichrist, as did the Maccabees as types of the faithful Christian. Thus he is of the lineage of the Devil....

Antiochus was always the descendant of the Devil, in his role of Antichrist; now [in the 12th-century commentary of Hugh of St. Victor] the allegory is carried further, and Alexander, as the historical predecessor of Antiochus and the originator of that division of the empire which made him king of Syria, is become the Devil....

[In an anecdote recounted by the 1st-century Jewish historian Josephus] Alexander, descending upon Jerusalem in wrath because a levy has been refused him, does obeisance to the High Priest who comes out with the assembled priesthood and people, in pursuance of a Divine injunction, to greet him. He does so because he reverences in the priest the earthly symbol of that God who had appeared to him in a dream, and told him that he would be assisted in his conquest of Persia and might rest assured of success. He was conducted into Jerusalem by the rejoicing Jews, is shown the prophecy of Daniel relating to him, and makes sacrifice in the Temple. On his departure he makes various concessions to Jerusalem

The image of an all-conquering Alexander riding roughshod over every foe has inspired ambitious men and women for centuries. Above: The triumphant Alexander, in marble, by the 17th-century French sculptor Pierre Puget.

and to the Jews in his empire....

In Antiquity the episode had been accepted by the Jews, who saw in Alexander a hero of their own. From them, through the agency of Josephus, it became known and approved by those who felt a similar admiration for Alexander.... [According to some medieval theologians] God worked upon Alexander to spare the Jews; his mercy shown towards Jerusalem was no act of devout reverence, but was due to a demonstration of God's power which compelled even him to obedience and recognition. The emphasis is on God's omnipotence over Alexander as over all tyrants. Alexander's dream is conveniently forgotten, and he appears as the instrument of God as in the Daniel prophecy—but an instrument which

turned awry. It was God's will that Alexander should destroy the Persians...but it was not God's will that Alexander should approach Jerusalem with wrath and vengeance in his heart, and he is deterred from his wicked purpose only by the especial prevision of God on behalf of the Jewish people, which made him appear to the High Priest, and tell him how he should act. In his attack upon Jerusalem Alexander is contravening the purpose of God, his destined task is not accomplished, the invasion of Persia not begun. But Jerusalem is hedged about with a divinity that impresses itself even upon *his* pagan heart, and he is forced into reverence....

The great popularity of the story of Alexander's entry into Jerusalem ensured its incorporation in many Alexander-books. Except in Germany, however, neither this nor the Daniel prophecy had any apparent effect upon the secular conception of Alexander. If it received any secular interpretation, it was the natural interpretation—that Alexander paid a due reverence to God, and thus showed himself humble.

We have here seen how the theologians built upon the basis of Orosius and the Bible an attack upon Alexander....

It is well known that many European churches contain representations of Alexander carried up into the sky in a chariot drawn by two or more gryphons, who are enticed upwards by bait spitted on the ends of two lances. This episode, borrowed in most cases probably from the *Historia de Preliis,* and frequently found on facades and misericords, has been long acknowledged to possess some symbolic significance. The exact nature of the symbolic interpretation intended has not yet been established, although many different theories have been produced, ranging from the interpretation of Alexander as Antichrist to the suggestion that the episode is symbolic of the Resurrection.

It seems necessary, however, to remark here that the literary treatment of the story of the Celestial Journey in Germany must automatically suggest that an unfavourable interpretation was attached to the representations of it in German churches, an interpretation which probably concurred with the theological condemnation of Alexander's pride....

The genesis of the theological approach to Alexander may be briefly stated. The prophecies of Daniel and the historical sketch of Maccabees were the foundation on which the theological writers built. By them Alexander was seen as the foreordained destroyer of Persia, and as the predecessor of Antiochus, the accepted type of Antichrist. In order to expand this Alexander portrait for purposes of Biblical commentary theologians turned to the life of Alexander in Orosius, the storehouse of ancient history for those who were neither humanists nor professional historians. And Orosius confirmed the conception of Alexander that was foreshadowed in his bare Biblical role as an instrument of wrath and as the ultimate cause of the reign of the anathematized Antiochus. He was a man of abominable pride, a pride so great that he might admirably symbolize the Devil. This conception of Alexander was first in the field. Already developed in Fulgentius and in St. Jerome, it established a prejudice that bore down all evidence favourable to Alexander and brought about his general condemnation.

Although this condemnation of Alexander was the work equally of French and German mystics, its effect in France was nullified for two centuries by the great force and pervasiveness of the courtly tradition, which made most French writers admirers of Alexander. But in Germany the courtly tradition was less influential; and it is significant that throughout the whole of German Alexander literature, from Rhabanus Maurus to the *Middle Low German Alexander,* the tendency was to consider the life of Alexander not as a separate biography but as a chapter in Biblical history, as an extended commentary upon the opening verses of Maccabees, or as the history of the founder of Daniel's third world-kingdom.

This historical tendency to place Alexander against his Biblical background is accompanied by a steady persistence of the theological condemnation of Alexander in Germany during the medieval period. That condemnation was sometimes faintly echoed elsewhere, in France and in England, during the later Middle Ages; but Germany remained always the staunchest upholder of this unfavourable Orosian attitude to Alexander, which made its way into even the most courtly and the most favourable of her Alexander poems.

George Cary,
The Medieval Alexander, 1987

If Alexander is seen in Western tradition as a great hero of antiquity, how is he remembered in the East? One of his most spectacular achievements was to reach the Ganges River and to conquer part of India, Yet an Indian scholar notes that little record of his presence remains in the ancient Vedic texts. Nor are the subtler cultural effects of his passage easy to identify.

The *Iliad* was Alexander's bedside reading, and the heroes of Troy his models. On landing in Asia, he hastened to pay tribute to his idol. This 18th-century painting by Hubert Robert imagines him among the tombs and temples of an imaginary Troy, standing before Achilles's grave.

Some writers have exaggerated the consequences of Alexander's invasion of India, while others have altogether denied it. We should make an effort to find out the truth. V. A. Smith writes, "India remained unchanged. The wounds of the battle were quickly healed; the ravaged fields smiled again as the patient oxen and no less patient husbandmen resumed their interrupted labours; and the place of the slain myriads were filled by the teeming swarms of a population, which knows no limit save those imposed by the cruelty of man, or the still more pitiless operations of nature. India was not hellenized. She continued to live her life of splendid isolation; and soon forgot the passing of the Macedonian storm. No Indian author, Hindu, Buddhist or Jain makes even the faintest allusion to Alexander or his deeds."... According to Smith, Alexander's campaign, although carefully designed to secure a permanent conquest, proved to be a brilliantly successful raid and left no mark on India, except the scars of bloody war....

It appears reasonable to assume that Alexander meant to rule his Indian conquests as integral parts of his empire. It is clear from the division of the country into Satrapies on the Persian model. The general took care to colonize the strategic points. Arrian's account enables us to distinguish five separate divisions of the conquered land. The first was Paropamisadai, ruled at first by Tyriespes and later by Oxyartes. The second was Taxila under Philip. To his charge was added all the territory up to Jhelum on the east and the confluence of Indus and the Chenab in the south. The third division was the extended dominion of Poros. The fourth was the Satrapy of Peithon, which covered the Indus valley, below the confluence, and last was the territory of Abhisara in Kashmir. We can be sure that if Alexander had lived his normal life[span], the connection of the Satrapies with the rest of his empire would have been maintained and developed....

Politically Alexander's invasion was of little value. When the second partition of the empire was effected at Triparadeisos in 321 BC, Antipater practically recognized the independence of India. Poros and Ambhi as a matter of form were given the charge of Indus valley and Punjab. Peithon was transferred to Archosia. India was abandoned by the Macedonian government in reality. Only Eudemos retained some authority in the Indus valley until about 317 BC, taking with him the war elephants of Poros, whom he had slain treacherously. In any case his dream of including Punjab and Sind in his world empire was doomed to disappointment....

Alexander's invasion promoted the political unification of the country. At this time North-western India was divided into a number of independent principalities. They were always at war with each other. Alexander's invasion left the warrior tribes weakened and broken.... In the words of Hemchandra Raychaudhuri, "Alexander's invasion produced one indirect result. It helped the cause of Indian unity by destroying the power of the petty states of north-west India...." The role of Ambhi does not recur in Indian history for the next fifteen centuries. Though India was not hellenized, there was quite active contact between India and the Hellenistic kingdoms. In the realms of art, currency and astronomy, India became a debtor. The silver coins of Sophytes with Greek legends and their Attic weight standard are among the earliest witnesses to this development....

Although the Greeks had known something of India before the invasion of Alexander, their knowledge was mostly of the nature of fantastic tales. Now for the first time Greeks and Indians came into close contact. It is quite clear from the classical accounts that the Greeks were impressed by what they saw of India. They much admired the courage of the Indian troops. On the European side Alexander's invasion brought a vast increase in the knowledge of India. [The historian J. W. Merindle] observes, "Not a few of Alexander's officers and companions were men of high attainments in literature and science and some of their number composed memoirs of his wars, in the course of which they recorded their impressions of India and the races by which they found it inhabited." It is said that Alexander discovered a new world. But we must remember that Greece and India had known each other centuries before through the medium of the Persian empire. Craterus in his journey from the Indus valley to Karmania followed an already established route. It opened up an alternative land route and solved the problem of easy overland communication with Europe. The circumnavigation of the coast by Nearchus gave Alexander a third line of communication by sea. And if he had lived, he might have been successful in retaining his hold upon the Punjab and the Sind.... The only permanent result of Alexander's campaign was that it opened up communication between Greece and India and paved the way for a more intimate intercourse between the two. But this was achieved at the cost of untold sufferings inflicted upon India.

B. C. Sinha,
Studies in Alexander's Campaigns,
1973

Alexander the tactician: The battle of Gaugamela

Among the set battles of Alexander against the Persian forces, that of Gaugamela is the best known. All the classical authors devoted long passages to describing the positions of the two armies before the battle and the movements of their various squadrons. The relative precision of these reports is due to the existence of a Persian document preserved by Aristobulus, one of the Companions of Alexander, and himself a historian. Nevertheless, there remain numerous discrepancies in the accounts, which have provided much food for debate among students of warfare in antiquity.

The battle itself was precipitated by Alexander's movement "toward the right" (or *as if* toward the right—the Greek phrase is ambiguous), which alarmed Darius, who was afraid that, if the Macedonian army reached the ground which had not been levelled by the Persians, his (supposed) advantage in weaponry, in the form of scythe-chariots, would be nullified. He therefore ordered the advance-guard of his left wing—probably the thousand Bactrian cavalry and the two thousand Scythian Massagetae [Quintus Curtius IV.12.6–7]—to ride around the Macedonian right wing, which Alexander was leading in person, and halt its march. This placed Alexander on the defensive, and, in order to regain the initiative, he detailed Menidas to charge the enveloping Persians. The counter-attack, however, failed, and Menidas' small force—a mere four hundred horsemen—was driven back in disorder by the superior weight of the enemy cavalry. Alexander now ordered a charge by Aretes' *prodromoi* and the Paeonians of Ariston, closely supported by Cleander's veteran mercenary infantry. As this second counterattack, carried out by far more formidable Macedonian units, was meeting with greater success than the first, Bessus, Darius' left wing commander, threw into the fray the remaining Bactrians, possibly as many as eight thousand in number. These were themselves repulsed (and their battle-formations broken) after a long, hard fight, culminating in a vigorous charge by the units of the Macedonian flank-guard. Meanwhile, the Persian scythe-chariots were demonstrating their ineffectiveness in a charge against the

Macedonian right centre. They were promptly routed by Balacrus' javelin-men and the remaining half of the Agrianian contingent, who had been stationed in a forward position in order to screen the Companions.

Now came the crisis of the battle as Alexander halted his lateral march and began a direct advance on the Persian positions. The movement of some cavalry, which Darius had told off to support the troops attempting the envelopment of the Macedonian right, had left a gap in the front line of the Persian left centre. It was towards this gap that Alexander, seizing the tactical initiative once more, now wheeled, and, making a wedge of the Companion cavalry and part of the infantry phalanx, led the attack in the direction of Darius himself. At this development, the Great King fled.

In my paper, "Grand Tactics at Gaugamela," I suggested that this evolution into wedge-formation, carried out only during the crisis of the battle, led to the Macedonian army being credited by both [Quintus] Curtius and Diodorus with a battle-line in oblique order from the very beginning of the action. The identity of the source, or sources, utilized by these two historians for their accounts of the battle is, as we have seen, a major *crux*, and need not concern us here. It is possible that Curtius and Diodorus both muddled their accounts of Gaugamela them-selves. However, it is more likely that they inherited an already defective tradition. Nor, indeed, is it hard to see how such an erroneous version got its start. It may, at first, have been a case of mere oversimplification. For, whatever its original tactical alignment, the front line of the Macedonian army was at

this stage actually advancing in oblique order. The wedge [cited by Arrian, III.14.2] was, it should be stressed, no mere metaphor, but rather a complex formation of units arranged *en échelon* (that is, with the front of each indi-vidual unit parallel to that of the enemy), in two oblique lines, slanting in opposite directions but meeting in a broad point. The left-hand side of this massive wedge was made up of the hypaspists and the *taxeis* of the *pezhetairoi* from as far left as (and including) that of Polyperchon, while the *ilai* of the Companion cavalry constituted both the much shorter right-hand limb and the broad apex of the formation. A sharper point was doubtless provided by the person and royal *ile* of Alexander himself, swinging leftward to assail Darius. At the same time, the flank-guard of the Macedonian right wing, also in oblique order, was swinging outward to the right in close combat with the Bactrian cavalry of Bessus. A military ignoramus, especially if he had not been present at the battle, might well have become obscure, or even genuinely confused, when endeav-ouring to describe so complicated a tactical situation.

In my earlier discussion of the battle, I argued that the ultimate source for the reference to Alexander's wedge was Ptolemy. However, as we have seen, Callisthenes, as Alexander's official historian, is a more probable primary source. With his attention focused on the actions of Alexander himself, Callisthenes may not have formed a very clear idea of what was going on elsewhere on the field—the coverage of the proceedings on the Macedonian left is certainly far from comprehensive—but it appears to be only thanks to him (and to Ptolemy and Arrian, who preserved his account, at least in outline) that a fully coherent reconstruction of Alexander's oblique order tactics, and hence of the decisive moment of the battle, can be made.

Meanwhile, in the centre, owing to both the pace of Alexander's advance

The dramatic and decisive battle of Gaugamela has captured the imagination of many an artist. Here, the French court painter Charles Le Brun has depicted the glorious victory of Alexander for another powerful conqueror with a strong sense of history: his patron, Louis XIV. For many later rulers, Alexander remained the model of the heroic, triumphant king, whose achievements both military and political remained unequaled. It is not surprising, then, that throughout Europe paintings of Alexander's battles were commissioned by popes, kings, and emperors to decorate their palaces.

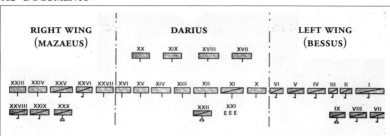

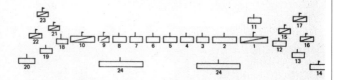

ALEXANDER

ORDERS OF BATTLE

THE MACEDONIAN ARMY

1. Companion cavalry (Philotas)
2. Hypaspists (Nicanor)
3–8. *Pezhetairoi* and *Asthetairoi* (regiments of Macedonian infantry)
9. Allied Greek cavalry (Erigyius)
10. Thessalian cavalry (Philip)
11. Agrianians, Archers, and Javelin-men (Balacrus)
12. Agrianians (Attalus)
13. Macedonian archers (Brison)
14. Old mercenary infantry (Cleander)
15. *Prodromi* (Aretes)
16. Paeonian cavalry (Ariston)
17. Mercenary cavalry (Menidas)
18. Thracian javelin-men (Sitalces)
19. Cretan archers
20. Achaean mercenary infantry
21. Allied Greek cavalry (Coeranus)
22. Odrysian cavalry (Agathon)
23. Mercenary cavalry (Andromachus)
24. Greek infantry

25. Thracian infantry, guarding the baggage-park

THE PERSIAN ARMY

A. Left Wing (Bessus):
   I. Bactrian cavalry (Bessus in person): ?8,000
  II. Dahae cavalry: 1,000
 III. Arachosian cavalry (?Barsaentes): ?2,000
 IV. Persian cavalry and infantry
  V. Susian cavalry: ?2,000
 VI. Cadusian cavalry: ?2,000
VII. Scythian cavalry: 2,000
VIII. Bactrian cavalry: 1,000
 IX. Scythe-chariots: 100

B. Centre (Darius in person):
  X. Greek mercenary infantry (?Paron): ?1,000
 XI. Kinsmen cavalry (with Darius): 1,000
XII. *Melophoroi*: ?1,000

XIII. Greek mercenary infantry
(?Glaucus): ?1,000
XIV. Indians
XV. Resettled Carians (?Bupares)
XVI. Mardian archers
XVII. Uxians (?Oxathres)
XVIII. Babylonians (?Bupares)
XIX. "Red Sea" Tribesmen (?Ocondobates,
Ariobarzanes, and Orxines)
XX. Sitacenians (?Bupares)
XXI. Elephants: 15
XXII. Scythe-chariots: 50

C. Right Wing (Mazaeus):
XXIII. Syrians and Mesopotamians
(Mazaeus in person)
XXIV. Medes (?Atropates)
XXV. Parthian and Sacae horse-archers
(?Mauaces)
XXVI. Tapurian and Hyrcanian cavalry
(?Phrataphernes)
XXVII. Albanians and Sacesinians
XXVIII. Armenian cavalry (?Orontes)
XXIX. Cappadocian cavalry (?Ariaces)
XXX. Scythe-chariots: 50

MOVEMENTS AND MANOEUVRES

A ... A. Enveloping movement by Scythian and
Bactrian cavalry; Counterattack and retreat of
Menidas.

B ... B. Counterattack of Aretes and Ariston;
Attack of main body of Bactrian cavalry.

C ... C. Attack and rout of Persian scythe-

chariots; Alexander's main attack in wedge-
formation.

D ... D. Mazaeus' attack on Macedonian left.

F ... F. Persian raid on Macedonian baggage-
park; Counterattack by Macedonian second-
line infantry.

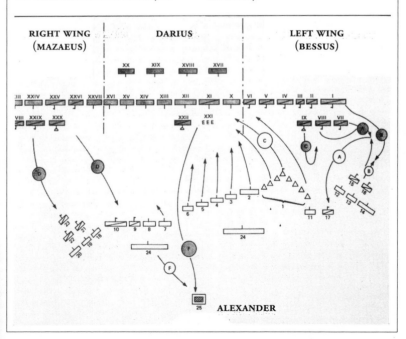

towards the gap in the Persian front and the evolution of his right into wedge-formation, a gap developed in the Macedonian army's own front line. While all the units from Polyperchon's *taxis* rightward surged forward in the great rupture of the Persian centre, Simmias, unable to push forward as rapidly, and learning that the left was in difficulties, halted his own *taxis* to succor it. Through the resultant gap there now penetrated a force of Indian and Persian cavalry from the disintegrating enemy centre. Reaching the Macedonian baggage-park, they fell upon its defenders, overwhelmed them, and liberated the prisoners they found there. At this, the Macedonian second-line infantry, in accordance with previous orders, faced about and put the raiders to flight.

While all this was taking place, the left, under the command of Parmenion, was sustaining an attempted envelopment, as well as a frontal assault, by the as yet undefeated Persian right under Mazaeus. Being thus hard-pressed, Parmenion despatched riders to Alexander, asking for assistance. It is almost certain, despite statements to the contrary in our sources, that this message was never delivered. For when Parmenion's messengers reached the Macedonian right, they found that Alexander was already far advanced in his all-out pursuit of Darius and returned without having accomplished their mission. Fortunately, however, for the Macedonian cause, Parmenion succeeded without help in checking the Persian attack with his Thessalian cavalry. Then, as news of the Great King's flight from the field filtered through to the faltering Persian right, the repulse quickly became a rout.

Whether or not he received Parmenion's appeal for help, Alexander *did* turn back, most probably because of the loss of Darius' trail at the Lycus (Great Zab) and the growing darkness of evening. It was during his rearward ride that Alexander became involved in a short but bloody clash with a large body of retreating Persian cavalry, in company with some Parthian and Indian horse. Here, according to Arrian, took place the hardest-fought cavalry action of the entire battle. Having slain sixty of Alexander's Companion cavalry and wounded his favourite Hephaestion, the remnants of the Persian horse broke through the Macedonian squadrons and made good their escape.

When he had assured himself of the fact that his army was completely victorious, and that there was hence no more glory to be won on the field, Alexander renewed his pursuit of Darius. Meanwhile, Parmenion advanced and took the Persian camp, along with the enemy's baggage-train and elephants. Having crossed the Lycus, Alexander bivouacked on the far side and rested his cavalry until around midnight, when he rode on to Arbela, some forty miles away, where he hoped to capture both Darius and his field-treasury. When he reached Arbela the following day, he did in fact find there the Persian field-treasury, as well as his defeated opponent's chariot, but no Darius. The Great King had ridden on to meet an ignominious end—at the hands of his own subjects.

A. M. Devine,
"The Battle of Gaugamela:
A Tactical and Source-Critical Study,"
The Ancient World,
August 1986

Vergina: The tomb of Philip II or Philip III?

The royal tombs found at Vergina in Macedonia contained splendid, precious objects of gold and silver, ivory and marble, and magnificent wall paintings. They also held several richly interred bodies, whose identities have been the subject of much discussion among archaeologists.

The reconstruction which seems best to fit the evidence at present available is as follows. In 370 Alexander II built Tomb I to receive the remains of Amyntas III, the first member of his side of the descent from Alexander I to become king; for that reason Alexander II chose a site apart from the tombs of earlier kings. Adjacent to the tomb he built a shrine, perhaps called the Amyntaeum as at Pydna, and worship of Amyntas as a god was practiced there. We do not know as yet whether Amyntas was cremated; the report of "many bones" suggests perhaps that he was not cremated and that others were buried there later.

In 336, after the assassination of Philip II, Alexander III [the Great] spent several weeks in organizing affairs in Macedonia and enquiring into the background of the assassination. Meanwhile some progress was made in the building of a tomb for Philip, which Alexander had planned to a size which no subsequent built-tomb in Macedonia achieved. The trial was held and the guilty were sentenced. Then "Alexander took all possible care of his father's funeral" (Diodorus Siculus, *Historical Library,* XVII.2.1), placing in the tomb offerings which were superb both in quality and quantity. The king's chamber was closed before its interior was fully finished, because Alexander had to hasten away and deal with conditions in the Greek states. His deputy supervised the completion of the ante-chamber, the placing of the queen's remains and the addition of many offerings. The assassin's spear and horses, and two "conspirators" were burnt upon the pyre, and the iron, bronze, ivory and gold pieces were laid in a brick tray above the vault. And on the cornice, where the assassin's corpse had hung and then been burnt, a small fire of purification was lit. Alexander chose to site this tomb close to Tomb 1, in order that the worship accorded to Philip as a god might be made at the shrine. Tombs 1 and 2, each having its own small tumulus which showed above ground level, were now covered with an extensive tumulus of red soil....

In 321, when the corpse of Alexander III was diverted to Egypt, the Macedonians probably placed trophies from Persia and statues of Alexander and his special commanders in a stoa constructed close to the tumulus of red soil. In 316, when Arrhidaeus, Eurydice and Cynna were killed, Cassander buried their remains in a tomb somewhere outside the periphery of the great Mound. In 310, when the last male of the line, Alexander IV, died, he was buried in a tomb which was placed within the circumference of the tumulus of red soil. After 336 and before 310 the corpses of two men, not cremated, and two funerary headstones were placed in the upper soil of this tumulus; it had no doubt been their wish to be associated with the dynasty of Amyntas.

After 310 worship ceased at the burnt area by the shrine. Then or later (a point which the complete excavation may have decided) a great Mound, such as Alexander had planned to commemorate Philip, was erected perhaps to commemorate the dynasty which had ended.

N. G. L. Hammond,
"The Evidence for the Identity of the Royal Tombs in Vergina,"
Collected Studies,
1993

But what of the burial site of Alexander the Great himself? No certain trace of it exists in modern Alexandria, but archaeologists continue to search.

Alexander the Great, dying at Babylon on the banks of the Euphrates River in June of 323 BC, was explicit in his last wish. He wanted his body thrown into the river so that his corpse would disappear. In that way, Alexander reasoned, his survivors might perpetuate the myth that he was whisked off to heaven in order to spend eternity at the side of the god Ammon, who had allegedly fathered him. His generals, not respecting the wish, concocted elaborate plans for his burial. According to one ancient account, it took two years from the time of Alexander's death to design and construct a suitable funerary cart in which his mummified

An ivory portrait head of Philip II, who may be buried at Vergina.

Excavations at Vergina revealed the site of Aegae, one of the early capitals of Macedonia. This was the traditional burial place of the Macedonian kings and royal families. It was the successor's duty to lead the funeral procession and preside over the burial in the tomb the late monarch had built for himself. This was, for example, Alexander's first task after the death of his father, Philip II.

body could be conveyed to its tomb. En route to its destination…[Ptolemy] diverted the body to Egypt where it was buried in a tomb at Memphis.

Subsequently, in the late fourth or early third century BC…the body of Alexander was removed from its tomb in Memphis and transported to Alexandria where it was reburied. At a still later date, Ptolemy Philopator (222/21–205 BC) placed the bodies of his dynastic predecessors as well as that of Alexander, all of which had apparently been buried separately, in a communal mausoleum in Alexandria. By now Alexander had had at least three tombs in two Egyptian cities. Whenever someone asks where the tomb of

Alexander the Great is located, I assume the query refers to the third and last tomb, although admittedly the question might apply equally to his tomb at Memphis or to his first Alexandrian tomb, neither of which has ever been found.

The literary tradition is clear that the third and last tomb was located at the crossroads of the major north-south and east-west arteries of Alexandria. Octavian, the future Roman Emperor Augustus, visited Alexandria shortly after the suicide of Cleopatra VII in 30 BC. He is said to have viewed the body of Alexander, placing flowers on the tomb and a golden diadem upon Alexander's mummified head. The last recorded visit to the tomb was made by the Roman Emperor Caracalla in AD 215. The tomb was probably damaged and perhaps even looted during the political disturbances that ravaged Alexandria during the reign of Aurelian shortly after AD 270. By the fourth century AD the tomb's location was no longer known, if one can trust the accounts of several of the early Church Fathers. Thereafter, creditable Arab commentators, including Ibn Abdel Hakam (AD 871), Al-Massoudi (AD 944), and Leo the African (sixteenth century AD) all report having seen the tomb of Alexander, but do not specify its exact location.

The Egyptian Antiquities Organization has officially recognized more than 140 searches for Alexander's tomb, and there have been at least four recent attempts to locate it [including a dig in downtown Alexandria]….

[This] excavation site abuts the Mosque of Nebi Daniel, where Arabic tradition maintains the tomb is to be found. In 1991 Mohammed Abduk Aziz

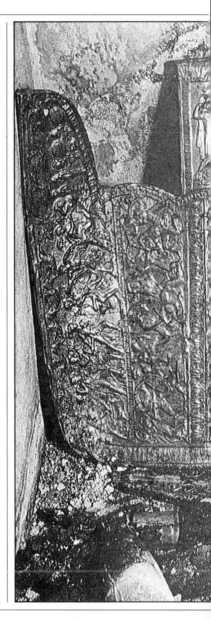

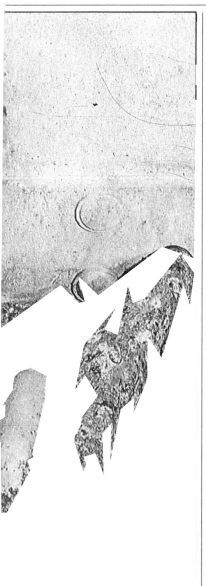

The royal tombs at Vergina held objects fit indeed for a king. Here, still in place in the antechamber of Tomb 2, is a rare gilded silver *gorytos*, or quiver, untouched by the centuries. Beside it lie gilded bronze greaves, or leg armor. The arms of the Macedonian kings were famous in their time for exceptional quality.

of the Arabic Language Department of Al Azhar University in Zagazig directed excavations at the mosque. He contends that Arabic sources, often overlooked by scholars searching for the tomb, offer good reasons for identifying the mosque with the tomb.... Religious officials charged with the administration of the mosque have obtained a moratorium on excavation, fearing that further digging might undermine the building's foundations and precipitate its collapse....

[Then] there is the claim of Stellio Komotsos, a Greek waiter in Christina Konstantinou's cafe-bar L'Élite in Alexandria. Obsessed with discovering the tomb, Komotsos would save every piaster he earned and, when not waiting tables, go off and dig holes everywhere he could in the city. Now retired and reportedly living in Athens, he is said to have amassed more notes, maps, and documentation on the subject than any scholar. Who knows what secrets are contained therein? Komotsos once offered to share his data with a patron in exchange for a pension in dollars and a new Mercedes. Such a price, mused one starry-eyed graduate student, would be small indeed if the key to the location of the tomb of Alexander was to be found in the Komotsos "archive"!

Robert S. Bianchi,
"Hunting Alexander's Tomb,"
Archaeology,
July–August 1993

Chronology

359 BC Philip II becomes king of Macedonia

356 c. 20 July Birth of Alexander, son of Philip

343 Aristotle becomes tutor to Alexander

340 Athens declares war against Macedonia. Alexander, regent of Macedonia while Philip is away at war, wins a battle in Thrace and founds a town, Alexandria, the first of many of that name

338 Battle of Chaeronea. Philip forms the Corinthian League of loyal Greek city-states. Alexander visits Athens as an ambassador in peace negotiations

336 Philip sends Macedonian forces to Asia in preparation for a larger expedition. Summer: Assassination of Philip. Alexander, age 20, accedes to the throne and is elected general of the Greeks by the Corinthian League. In Persia, Darius II becomes Great King

335 Spring–summer: Campaigns of Alexander on the frontiers of Macedonia. Autumn: He suppresses a revolt of Greek cities. Destruction of Thebes

334 Spring: Alexander invades Asia. First victory over Persians at the battle of Granicus. Summer: Cities on the coast of Asia Minor submit to Alexander. Winter: Conquests in southern Asia Minor (Lycia, Pamphylia, Phrygia); Miletus and Halicarnassus fall. Alexander winters at Gordium, in Phrygia.

Episode of the Gordian Knot

333 Spring: Alexander advances on Cilicia. The Persians, under Memnon, counterattack by sea and are defeated. 1 November: First set battle between Alexander and the Persian Great King Darius, at Issus; defeat of Darius, who flees back to Babylon. Winter: Alexander subdues most of Phoenicia and invades Egypt

332 January: Fall of Sidon. 29 July: Fall of Tyre. September: Fall of Gaza. 14 November: Alexander enthroned as Pharaoh at Memphis.

331 Alexander occupies all of Egypt. Expedition to the oracle of Ammon at Siwah; he is proclaimed divine. 7 April: Founds Alexandria. 1 October: Second victory of Alexander over Darius, at the battle of Gaugamela. The Great King flees east. October–December: Alexander occupies Babylon, Susa, and Persepolis

330 January–May: Alexander destroys the palace at Persepolis in May. Darius retreats toward Bactria. Summer: Alexander pursues Darius, occupying Media and Parthia. July: Assassination of Darius by Persians. Alexander has him buried with honors at Persepolis. Alexander begins to adopt Persian court ceremonial. Autumn:

Alexander suppresses the revolt of Satibarzanes, satrap of Aria. Philotas, a Macedonian noble, and Parmenio, a Macedonian general under Alexander, are accused of treason and executed

329 Spring: After great difficulties, Alexander's army crosses the Hindu Kush and arrives at Bactria, where the satrap Bessus has assumed the title of Great King. Summer: Alexander crosses the Oxus (Amu Darya) River and enters Bactria, taking and executing Bessus. He advances to Maracanda (Samarkand)

328 Summer: A difficult campaign in Sogdiana. Alexander murders Cleitus. A treason plot against Alexander is sparked by his order that Macedonians perform obeisance before him. Execution of the leader, Callisthenes. Winter: Alexander marries the Sogdian Roxane.

327 Spring: The army invades India. Autumn: It proceeds in two units to the Hydaspes (Indus) River

326 Summer: Defeat of the rajah Porus of India. Autumn: At the Hyphasis (Beas) River, Alexander's soldiers refuse to go farther. Reluctantly, Alexander turns back. November: Alexander defeats the Malavas. Winter: Brahmin cities are attacked; Alexander is

wounded, but recovers

325 January–July: The army rests at Pattala (Hyderabad?), on the Indus delta, and founds a port and shipyard, to construct ships. Alexander's general Craterus and some troops travel overland through the Bolan Pass and Kandahar. August: Alexander crosses Gedrosia (Baluchistan). September: Departure of the new fleet with a part of the army, under the command of the Macedonian Nearchus. They travel west along the coast of the Persian Gulf. December: Nearchus and Alexander meet in Carmania; Alexander continues on to Persia

324 January: Alexander restores the tomb of the Persian king Cyrus the Great at Pasargadae. February: At Susa, in a mass wedding, Macedonian nobles marry Persian brides. Summer: Alexander resides at Ecbatana. Death of Hephaistion. Campaign against the Cossaeans

323 Spring: Returning to Babylon, Alexander builds a fleet in preparation for an expedition to Arabia. 13 June: Death of Alexander. His general Perdiccas takes power in Asia

322 Alexander's empire fragments as Perdiccas, Ptolemy, Antipater, Seleucus, and other Macedonian generals divide it into satrapies and spheres of power

Further Reading

PRINCIPAL ANCIENT
SOURCES

Arrian, *Anabasis [Campaigns] of Alexander*, 1989.

Diodorus Siculus [Diodorus of Sicily], *Historical Library*, 1963, 1984.

Justin [Marcus Junianus Justinus], *Epitome of the Phillipic History of Pompeius Trogus*, n.d.

Nizam Nizami, *The Sikander Nama: E Bara, or Book of Alexander the Great Written AD 1200*, n.d.

Plutarch, "Life of Alexander the Great," in *Lives of the Noble Grecians and Romans*, 1992, and "On the Fortune or the Virtue of Alexander," in *Moralia*, 1972.

Quintus Curtius [Rufus], *History of Alexander*, 2 vols., 1946.

MODERN WORKS

Bieber, M., *Alexander the Great in Greek and Roman Art*, 1964.

Bosworth, A. B., *Conquest and Empire: The Reign of Alexander the Great*, 1993.

Burn, Andrew R., *Persia and the Greeks: The Defense of the West*, 1984.

Cary, George, *The Medieval Alexander*, 1987.

Ehrenberg, Victor, *Alexander and the Greeks*, 1985.

Green, Peter, *Alexander of Macedon: 356–323 BC, A Historical Biography*, 1991.

—, *Alexander to Actium: The Evolution of the Hellenistic Age*, 1994.

Griffith, G. T., ed., *Alexander the Great: The Main Problems*, 1966.

Hammond, N. G. L., *A History of Greece*, 2d ed., 1967.

Milns, R. D., *Alexander the Great*, 1968.

O'Brien, John M., *Alexander the Great: The Invisible Enemy, a Biography*, 1992.

Olmstead, A. T., *A History of the Persian Empire*, 1948.

Pearson, Lionel, "The Diaries and Letters of Alexander the Great," *Historia* 3 (1954–55), 429–55.

Renault, Mary, *Fire from Heaven*, 1969.

—, *The Persian Boy*, 1972.

—, *Funeral Games*, 1981.

—, *The Nature of Alexander*, 1975.

Stein, Marc Aurel, *On Alexander's Track to the Indus*, 1974.

Stoneman, Richard, trans. and ed., *The Greek Alexander Romance*, 1991.

Tarn, William W., *Alexander the Great*, 2 vols., 1948.

Wilcken, Ulrich, *Alexander the Great*, 1967.

List of Illustrations

Index

Acknowledgments

Thanks are due to the following persons and organizations for assistance in the publication of the present work: Monique Kervran and Jean Perrot for the photograph of the statue of Darius (p. 23); the Bibliothèque d'Assyriologie, Collège de France, and M. Dussaud; John Bastias and Ekdotike Publishers, Athens; the photographers Jean-Loup Charmet, François Delebecque, and Pierre Pitrou. Picture rights: Edith Garraud; layout: Francesco Moretti; maps: Patrick Mérienne.

Photograph Credits

Alexander's Celestial Journey, 1506, woodcut from a Renaissance-era Alexander romance, reproduced from George Cary, *The Medieval Alexander*, New York, 1987 154. Alinari/Viollet, Paris 38, 118, 155. All rights reserved spine, 15a, 26, 27, 30, 31, 37b, 44–45, 46, 61, 71, 72–73, 78, 78–79, 86–87, 92b–93, 116–17b, 117a, 141, 148. Artephot/Ziolo, Paris 32–33, 89a. Bibliothèque de l'Institut, Paris 120, 127, 143a. Bibliothèque Nationale, Paris 14–15, 36, 41, 42a, 74–75, 80, 81, 84, 108, 109, 126a, 130, 135, 147, 150. Bildarchiv Preussischer Kulturbesitz, Berlin 121, 128, 139. Bridgeman Art Library, London 54–55. British Museum, London 103, 132. Bulloz, Paris 24–25, 65, 67b, 104b, 105, 113, 151. Canali, Rome front cover. Jean-Loup Charmet, Paris 28–29. Peter Clayton, London 11l, 11r, 45a, 48l, 58, 59, 66b, 83b, 104a, 126c. Dagli-Orti, Paris 10, 16al, 16b–17b, 18, 34, 39, 48r, 106, 110b, 115a, 115b, 122–23, 124a, 124b, 125, 166. Editions du Cercle d'Art, Paris 88–89. Ekdotike, Athens 9, 16ac, 16ar, 17a, 19a, 19b, 21, 37a, 56–57, 64, 95, 96b–97, 167, 168–69. Explorer, Paris 60, 102. Giraudon, Paris 62–63, 143b. R. and S. Michaud, Paris 76, 77, 86, 92a, 96a, 99. Musée des Beaux-Arts, Lille 100–101. Musée de Brou, Bourg-en-Bresse, France 1, 2–3, 4–5, 6–7. Jean Perrot, Paris 23c. Pucciarelli, Rome 12b–13. Roger-Viollet, Paris 42–43, 133, 134, 137, 146. Réunion des Musées Nationaux, Paris 35, 66a–67a, 68, 69, 107, 112, 138, 157, 161. Scala, Florence 20, 47, 51, 52–53, 90–91. Diagrams from A. M. Devine, "The Battle of Gaugamela: A Tactical and Source-Critical Study," *The Ancient World*, August 1986, Copyright © 1986 *The Ancent World*, Ares Publishers, Inc. 162, 163.

Text Credits

Grateful acknowledgement is made for use of material from the following: Arrian, *Anabasis of Alexander*, Book I, trans. P. A. Brunt, Loeb Classical Library, Cambridge, Mass.: Harvard University Press, 1989 (pp. 131, 132); Robert Bianchi, "Hunting Alexander's Tomb," *Archaeology* 46. no. 4 (July–August 1993), Reprinted with the permission of *Archaeology Magazine*, Copyright the Archaeological Institute of America, 1993 (pp. 166–69); George Cary, *The Medieval Alexander*, New York: Garland, 1987 (pp. 152–56); A. M. Devine, "The Battle of Gaugamela: A Tactical and Source-Critical Study," *The Ancient World*, August 1986, Copyright © 1986 *The Ancient World*. Reprinted by permission of Ares Publishers, Inc. (pp. 159–64); Diodorus of Sicily, Books XVII, XVIII, XIX, trans. C. Bradford Welles and Russel M. Geer, Loeb Classical Library, Cambridge, Mass.: Harvard University Press, 1963, 1984, © The President and Fellows of Harvard College 1963 (pp. 133, 141, 142–43, 144–45); *The Greek Alexander Romance*, Richard Stoneman, Book III, New York: Penguin Books USA, 1991, Copyright © Richard Stoneman, 1991 (pp. 151–52); *Alexander the Great*, by J. R. Hamilton, © 1973. Reprinted by permission of the University of Pittsburgh Press (pp. 149–51); N. G. L. Hammond, "The Evidence for the Identity of the Royal Tombs in Vergina," *Collected Studies*, Adolf M. Hakkert, Amsterdam, 1993 (pp. 165–66); Plutarch, "Life of Alexander," "Life of Demetrius," *Lives of the Noble Grecians and Romans*, trans. John Dryden, New York: Modern Library, 1992; Plutarch, "On the Fortune or the Virtue of Alexander," *Moralia*, vol. 4, trans. Frank Cole Babbitt, Loeb Classical Library, Cambridge, Mass.: Harvard University Press, 1972 (pp. 132–33, 134–35, 147–48); Quintus Curtius, *History of Alexander*, Book X, trans. John C. Rolfe, Loeb Classical Library, Cambridge, Mass.: Harvard University Press, 1976 (p. 142); B. C. Sinha, *Studies in Alexander's Campaigns*, Varanasi, India: Bhartiya Publishing House, 1973 (pp. 157–58).

Pierre Briant
teaches ancient history at the University of Toulouse.
A specialist in the history of the Mideast under the
Persians and after Alexander's conquests, he is
the author of an account of Antigonus the One-Eyed
(one of Alexander's successors) and of many articles
and books. These include *Alexander le Grand*,
1987; *Rois, Tributs et Paysans*, 1982; and
The State and the Shepherd, 1982.

© Gallimard 1987

English translation © Harry N. Abrams, Inc.,
New York, 1996

Translated from the French by Jeremy Leggatt

A catalogue record for this book is available
from the British Library

ISBN 0-500-30070-4

Printed and bound in Italy
by Editoriale Libraria, Trieste